REWILD
OF SELF

A Guided Companion
for Reconnection

Leanne Murner

Book layout: Planetary Press and Publishing Pty Ltd
Cover design: © Alethea Ruth Clair Aquilina
Interior artwork: © Alicia Phuntsok
Printed in Australia

ISBN: 978-0-6456435-7-2 (sc)
ISBN: 978-0-6456435-8-9 (e)

INTRODUCTION

Since the rise of technology, our lives have become faster, louder, and more fragmented. Information flows at a pace our minds were never designed to handle. Our attention is constantly pulled by devices, notifications, and screens, leaving little room for rest, reflection, or deep thinking. Over time, this constant stimulation can contribute to stress, anxiety, and a sense of disconnection, not just in adults, but especially in young people.

At the same time, many of us are spending less time outdoors. Nature, with all its rhythms, textures, and life, has become background or entirely absent from our daily routines. Yet research is clear: even brief exposure to natural environments, walking through a forest, sitting beside water, or even looking at an image of green hills can reduce stress, increase creativity, and promote a sense of calm and happiness. The effects grow stronger with consistent engagement, and the benefits can last days or even weeks.

There is another, perhaps deeper, benefit. When we take time to notice and connect with nature, we develop a sense of care and reciprocity. By recognising our place in the living world, we naturally act with more respect and attention. The relationship becomes mutually nourishing as nature supports us, and we support nature.

Rewild of Self is designed to help you cultivate these connections. Through simple, thoughtful practices, this journal will guide you in slowing down, noticing, and interacting with the world around you. It is not about perfection or following strict rules; it is about exploring and finding what works best for you. Each Practise, reflection, and prompt is a gentle invitation to pause, breathe, and reconnect with yourself, the environment, and the rhythms of life, picking what resonates along your journey.

Finding Your Centre

Before beginning, it's helpful to set aside a few minutes to calm your mind and reconnect with your breath. This prepares you to fully experience and enjoy the exercises.

Some simple practices include:

- **Breath Awareness:** Close your eyes and bring your attention to your breathing. Notice the natural flow, inhale… exhale… inhale… exhale. Repeat for a few minutes, allowing your mind to settle.
- **Naming Your Breath:** As you inhale, silently say "in," and as you exhale, silently say "out." Continue until you feel a sense of calm.
- **Subtle Observation:** Pay attention to the movement of air through your nose. Is one nostril more active than the other? Does the sensation change? There is no right or wrong, the intention is simply to notice.

Other ways to gently prepare include feeling your feet on the ground, listening to surrounding sounds, or lightly stretching to release tension. The goal is simple: to create a space of presence, where your mind is allowed to rest, reboot, and settle into the rhythms of your own body.

Once you feel centred, you are ready to explore the practices in this book. Each Practise will guide you through experiences in nature and at home, helping you reawaken your senses, nurture creativity, and strengthen your connection to the living world.

Before you begin, take a moment to choose a special journal, perhaps a favourite one you already have, or a new notebook dedicated to this journey. Use it to record your reflections, sketches, and discoveries as you move through each practice. This will become your personal record of reconnection, a space where your thoughts, emotions, and experiences in nature unfold and take shape.

Take your time. There is no rush. Every page, every practice, is a chance to pause, breathe, and reconnect. Trust that you will be drawn to what resonates with you in that moment.

Gentle Tips for Beginners to Journaling / Creative Writing

- Short is okay: Even setting aside 3–5 minutes counts.
- Engage curiosity over judgment: Don't be hard on yourself if your mind wanders, gently bring attention back through breath.
- Consistency matters more than duration: Daily small practices build awareness more than rare long sessions.
- No prior knowledge is required: Just notice what feels present or absent.
- Don't force it: It's ok if nothing comes, that may just be what you need in that moment.
- All imagination counts, there's no right or wrong way to express yourself, and no right or wrong way to write. Simply begin where you are and write what first comes to mind. You might be quite surprised by what surfaces, memories, feelings, or ideas that have been quietly waiting beneath the surface, perhaps ones you haven't visited in a long time.
- As you move through these nature-based practices, you'll be invited to explore your creativity through reflection, writing, and

storytelling. Notice what stories arise from your experiences, the ones nature whispers to you, the ones that have shaped you, or perhaps the ones you're ready to tell for the first time.

Exploring Nature Through Journaling and Creative Writing

This is your space to explore how nature and imagination intertwine, helping you rediscover your voice, your rhythms, and your connection to the world around you. Through journaling and creative expression, you begin to see how your inner landscape mirrors the patterns of the natural world.

Each entry is an invitation to slow down, notice, and express what's unfolding both within and around you.

Tips for Beginners

- Start simple: Begin with what catches your attention: a leaf, a sound, a feeling, or a memory. Let it guide your writing.

- Reflect on meaning: Notice what insights, emotions, or patterns your stories and reflections reveal.

- Write freely: Don't overthink. Let words, sketches, or fragments flow without judgment or structure.

- Use your senses: Describe what you see, hear, smell, or feel, your senses are the bridge between you and the natural world.

- Be playful: Storytelling and journaling are about exploration, not perfection. Allow curiosity to lead.

- Follow your curiosity: If something in nature draws your attention, let it spark your creative process, a phrase, a drawing, a poem, or a scene.

- Write what comes first: There's no right or wrong way. Often, the first thoughts that surface hold hidden wisdom or long-forgotten feelings.

- Pause and breathe: Before you write, take a few slow, mindful breaths to centre yourself. Let your body settle before your pen begins to move.

- Use your journal as a companion: Choose a notebook that feels special, one that invites you to return to it. This is your space to grow, reflect, and create.

- Notice your patterns: Over time, you may see themes emerge, seasons of emotion, cycles of inspiration, or the echoes of nature mirrored in your life.

- Mix mediums: Try different forms of creative expression, journaling, poetry, drawing, or even movement. Each one reveals something new.

- Revisit your entries: Come back later to reflect. You may find deeper meanings or new perspectives waiting for you.

<u>Understanding Energy in the Body</u>

Within your body, there are natural areas where energy gathers, moves, and flows. You may not have been taught about them before, but you've likely felt them as a tight chest when you're overwhelmed, a flutter in your stomach when something doesn't feel right, or a lightness when you feel calm and open.

These areas are often referred to as energy centres. You don't need to remember their names or learn anything complicated, this is simply about becoming aware of how your body feels.

You can think of these centres as gentle points of awareness within your body, such as:

- **Your head** – where thoughts, clarity, and focus live.
- **Your throat** – where expression and communication flow.
- **Your chest/heart** – where emotions and connection are felt.
- **Your belly** – where intuition and instinct arise.
- **Your lower body** – where you feel grounded, stable, and supported.

At times, these areas may feel open, calm, and flowing. At other times, they may feel tight, heavy, or blocked.
Just like nature, your body moves in cycles. Energy shifts, changes, and responds to your environment, your thoughts, and your experiences.

When you slow down and bring gentle awareness to your body, you begin to notice these shifts. Through that awareness, things can begin to soften, open, and move more freely.
You don't need to force or fix anything, just noticing the signs is where the change begins.

VIII

Be sure to subscribe to my YouTube channel, you'll find a collection of guided meditations and writing sessions, these have been designed to help quiet the mind and support you along your journey.

These sessions can also be used alongside the practices in this book or whenever you feel the need for a quiet, guided space to write.

I share parts of my own story and unfolding path, a space where you can follow along, connect and reflect as you move through your own reconnection.

Wherever you are, and however you choose to explore this work, know that you are supported.

You can follow me by scanning the QR code below.

X

X

Dedication

I, too, have known what it feels like to be disconnected and unsure how to find my direction and quiet my mind to hear the messages.

I want to dedicate this to everyone that has crossed my path along my journey. Through shared moments, I have come to understand the depth of disconnection, conditioning, and programming that so many of us carry without any awareness.

Without those experiences, this book would not exist. It has opened my eyes to how deeply this reconnection is needed.

Through these practices they guided my pathway back within myself. Journaling is now apart of my every day, it allows the noise to soften, listen to the messages coming in and reconnecting into where I am being lead.

We all hold that power within us, we just need the space and the tools to remember it.

What is it you are seeking?

Happy writing.

Leanne

xx

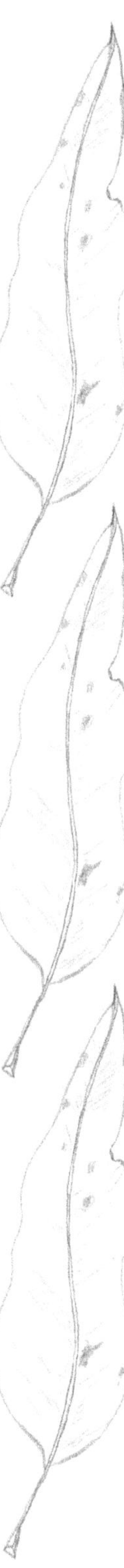

TABLE OF CONTENTS

TABLE OF CONTENTS

REWILD of self

TABLE OF CONTENTS

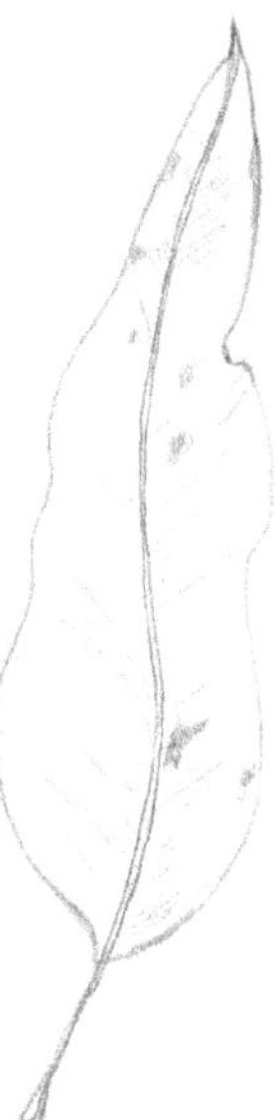

Practice 1 – The Pulse of the Living Earth

Re-synchronising with planetary rhythms, awareness of cycles, time, and rest

Many of us live lives that feel rushed, fractured, or disconnected from the natural world. We follow clocks and schedules, rarely noticing the small rhythms around us: the way the sun rises, the breeze moves, or the birds sing. Yet because we are part of the natural world, the pulses of the living Earth are mirrored in our own systems, if we allow ourselves to notice and tune into them.

This Practice is about slowing down and beginning to observe the patterns and cycles of life both outside and within yourself. These are the gentle pulses of the living Earth, and by tuning in, you can start to feel grounded, present, and aligned with your own inner rhythms.

For someone who has never practised nature-based reflection, it can feel strange at first to "sit and do nothing" or simply notice small things. But these simple acts allow your nervous system to calm, your senses to awaken, and your awareness to expand. You don't need to understand everything immediately. The key is presence and curiosity.

Over time, noticing natural rhythms can help you:

- Reduce stress and mental chatter.

- Feel more connected to the world around you.

- Understand your own patterns of energy, rest, and creativity.

- Begin cultivating a sense of belonging in the larger web of life.

In-Nature Practice - Feeling the Pulse with Breath

Feeling the Pulse will connect your body to the Earth's rhythm through simple, sensory awareness.

- Find a quiet spot outdoors. If possible, stand barefoot or sit on grass, soil, or sand. If you can't go outside, a balcony, garden, or even a sunny window works.

- Close your eyes and notice your breath. Don't change it, just feel it.

- Sense the temperature of the ground beneath your feet. Is it warm or cool? Firm or soft?

- Listen carefully. Notice one sound that repeats, a bird call, the rustle of leaves, wind through branches. Focus on it for a few breaths.

- When you are ready, gently open your eyes and write down what you noticed: the textures, temperatures, sounds, or feelings that emerged.

At-Home Practice - Mapping Your Daily Light with Breath

Mapping Your Daily Light, notice the natural rhythms indoors and connect them to your own energy.

- For a week, observe how light enters your home. Notice when the first rays of sun touch your space and when the light fades.
- Create a simple visual map of your day, you can use a drawing, a line chart, or even simple symbols. Include:
  - Times of high energy.
  - Times of fatigue.
  - Moments when you notice nature (sunlight, wind, birds.)
- Reflect on patterns: Do certain times feel energising? Do you feel more awake when the sun is up or after dusk?

Journaling Prompts - Exploring Your Rhythms

Where do I resist the natural flow of rest and renewal?

What time of day do I feel most alive, and what might that reveal about my internal seasons?

What small signs from nature can I notice today to reconnect to nature or self?

When do I feel most aligned with life's natural rhythm?

Which areas of my life feel forced rather than flowing?

How can I honour rest without guilt?

Where do I resist change or the natural cycles around me?

Practice 2 – Elements as Mirrors of the Self

Exploring inner temperament through Earth, Air, Fire, Water, and Aether

Nature offers us a language to understand ourselves and the elements. Earth, Air, Fire, Water, and Aether are powerful mirrors of inner qualities. Earth teaches stability, Air inspires clarity, Fire sparks passion, Water encourages flow, and Aether reminds us of spaciousness.

If you've never considered yourself in relation to the elements, it may feel abstract at first. This Practice helps you observe, reflect, and connect with the qualities you naturally express or avoid. By exploring the elements in nature, you can gain insight into your personality, moods, and creative energy.

Noticing elemental qualities helps you:

- Recognise your strengths and tendencies.
- Understand areas of imbalance or resistance.
- Cultivate a more harmonious inner life.
- Engage creatively with your environment.

In-Nature Practice - Observing the Elements

Explore the qualities of each element through sensory awareness.

- Choose one element each day to focus on:
    - Earth: Touch soil, rocks, or sand.
    - Air: Feel the wind, notice breezes.
    - Fire: Observe sunlight, warmth, or a flame safely.
    - Water: Watch a stream, rain, or puddle.
    - Aether: Notice open sky, spaciousness, or quiet air.
- Spend 5-10 minutes observing the chosen element. Notice:
    - How it feels physically (texture, temperature, movement.)
    - What qualities it seems to express (strength, fluidity, clarity, etc.)
- Speak aloud or think about what the element appears to teach you.
- Write down your reflections in your journal.

At-Home Practice - Creating an Elemental Altar

Engage with the elements using objects from your environment to inspire reflection.

- Gather one object for each element:
  - Earth: stone, soil, plant.
  - Air: feather, incense.
  - Fire: candle, picture of a sunrise, incense.
  - Water: bowl of water, cup of tea, river rock.
  - Aether: empty space, star chart, open sky image.
- Arrange them in a small area to create a visual and tactile altar.
- Sit with the altar for a few minutes, noticing the qualities each element represents.
- Journal your impressions and insights daily for a week to see how different things come up.

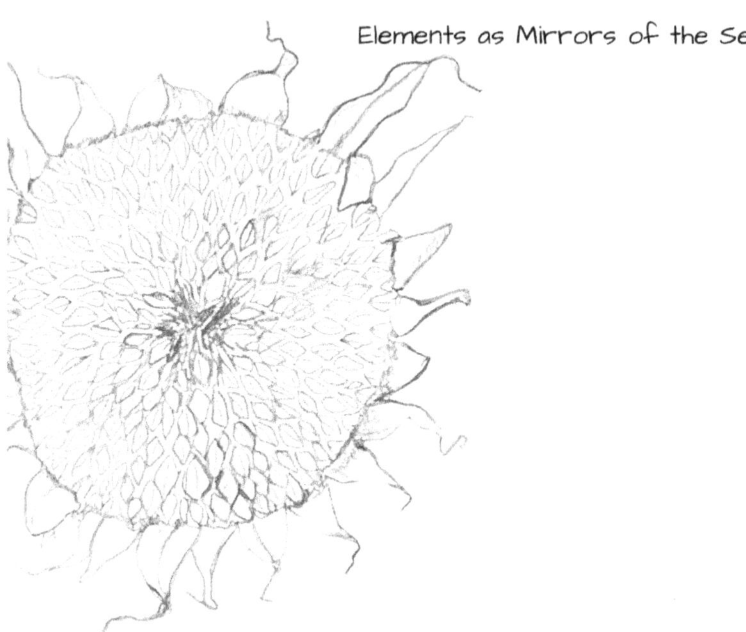

Journaling Prompts - Exploring Your Elements

Which element feels overexpressed in me right now?

Which element do I avoid or feel disconnected from?

How can I balance the qualities of each element in my daily life?

What do the elements teach me about my emotions and habits?

Which element feels strongest in me today, and why?

Where might I need more balance between the elements?

What lessons can I learn from the element I avoid?

Practice 3 – Silence and the Field

Listening beyond noise; rediscovering stillness as a living presence

In our modern world, we are surrounded by constant noise, from devices, traffic, or even our own thoughts. Silence is not simply the absence of sound; it is a living space where awareness can expand, and subtle patterns of life become visible.

For someone new to nature-based reflection, sitting in silence may feel uncomfortable or unfamiliar. This Practise invites you to slow down, notice what emerges, and connect more deeply with your environment and yourself. Even brief moments of stillness can reveal insights, emotions, or sensations you might normally overlook.

Practising silence helps you:

- Improve focus and clarity.
- Calm mental chatter and reduce stress.
- Heighten awareness of subtle natural patterns.
- Experience a sense of presence and inner stillness.

<u>In-Nature Practice - Silent Walk</u>

- Choose a quiet path, garden, or park for a short walk.
- Leave devices and distractions behind. Walk slowly and deliberately, noticing each step.
- Pay attention to textures, colours, shapes, sounds, and smells, observe without labelling or judging.
- Notice thoughts as they arise, then gently return focus to your surroundings.
- After your walk, sit or stand quietly and write in your journal about your sensory experience.

<u>At-Home Practice - Listening Meditation</u>

- Sit comfortably in a quiet room. Close your eyes if it feels safe.
- Focus on ambient sounds - ticking clocks, distant traffic, wind through a window.
- Notice the texture, tone, and rhythm of each sound. Let them pass without judgment.
- After 5-10 minutes, open your eyes and journal about what you noticed.

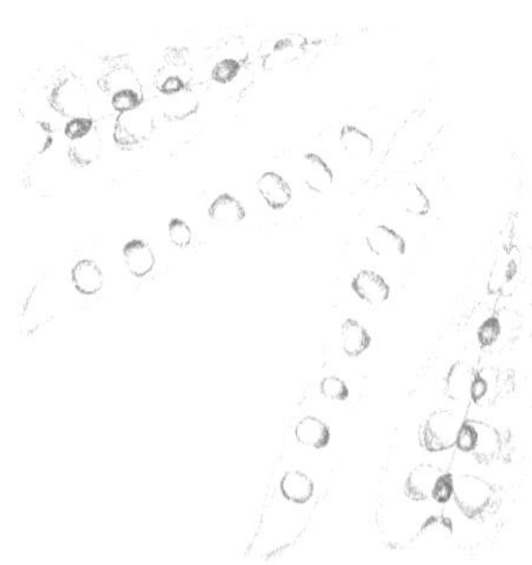

Journaling Prompts - Discovering Silence

What does silence reveal that noise hides?

When do I most resist stillness, and why?

How can I incorporate moments of silence into my daily life?

What patterns or details do I notice when I truly stop and pay attention?

What emerges in the quiet that I usually miss?

Which thoughts or emotions surface when I pause completely?

What does deep listening teach me about myself?

Practice 4 – Cycles of Light and Shadow

Integrating duality, learning from contrast and change

Life is full of cycles: day and night, growth and rest, joy and sorrow. Light and shadow are not opposites but companions, each teaching important lessons. By observing these natural rhythms, you can begin to understand your own inner cycles and appreciate the balance that emerges from contrast.

For beginners, noticing light and shadow can be a simple but powerful way to become more aware of impermanence, change, and the interplay between practice and rest.

Observing cycles of light and shadow helps you:

- Understand your own emotional and energetic patterns.
- Develop patience and acceptance of change.
- Recognise that contrast is necessary for growth and insight.
- Cultivate mindfulness in everyday life.

In-Nature Practice - Observing Light and Shadow

Notice how change and contrast appear in nature and reflect on your own life cycles.

- Choose a location you can observe over time, such as a tree, garden, or a spot in the park.
- Visit it at dawn and dusk, noticing differences in light, colour, and mood.
- Observe your own responses to the changing light. Does it energise, calm, or shift your feelings?
- Sit quietly and write down your observations, focusing on contrasts, transitions, and patterns.

At-Home Practice - Shadow and Light Reflection

Explore inner contrast through creative observation indoors.

- Light a candle or position a lamp to create shadows on a wall.
- Observe how the shapes and edges change as you move or as the flame flickers.
- Consider aspects of yourself you might be hiding (shadow) and those you express freely (light.)
- Journal your reflections, noting contrasts and what you might learn from them.

Journaling Prompts - Learning from Cycles

How do I honour my own darkness as well as my light?

Which parts of myself am I hiding from others or myself?

What am I hiding that wishes to be integrated?

What patterns of change do I notice in my life?

How can I embrace impermanence and transitions more fully?

What strengths have I found in my 'shadow' qualities?

What cycles in my life repeat, and what can I learn from them?

Practice 5 – Breath and Electric Life

Breath as the bridge between mind and nature's current

Breath is life. It is the invisible current that moves through us, connecting our inner world to the natural rhythms around us. Like wind through the trees or waves in the sea, your breath is a subtle but powerful force that reflects the flow of energy in your body and mind.

For someone new to these practices, focusing on breath can feel simple, yet it provides a tangible way to connect with yourself and the environment. By observing your breathing patterns and noticing how they respond to nature, you begin to understand your own inner currents and rhythms.

Paying attention to breath helps you:
- Ground yourself in the present moment.
- Increase awareness of your body and energy.
- Support emotional balance and calm.
- Connect your personal rhythm to the natural world.

<u>In-Nature Practice - Breathing with the World</u>

Sync your breath with natural movements to feel connection and flow.

- Choose a location outdoors where you can sit or stand comfortably.
- Close your eyes and notice your natural breathing. Don't try to change it.
- Observe natural movements around you: wind in the trees, waves, rustling leaves.
- Begin to match your breath to these movements: inhale as the wind rises, exhale as it falls; inhale as a wave swells, exhale as it retreats.
- After a few minutes, open your eyes and journal what you noticed about your body, mind, and connection to nature.

<u>At-Home Practice - Breath Awareness Practice</u>

Notice and reflect on your breath indoors to foster awareness and calm.

- Sit comfortably in a quiet space.
- Close your eyes and take a few moments to observe your natural breath.
- Try a simple pattern if it feels comfortable: inhale for four counts, pause briefly, exhale for four counts.
- Reflect on sensations in your body, energy shifts, and emotional responses.
- Journal your observations.

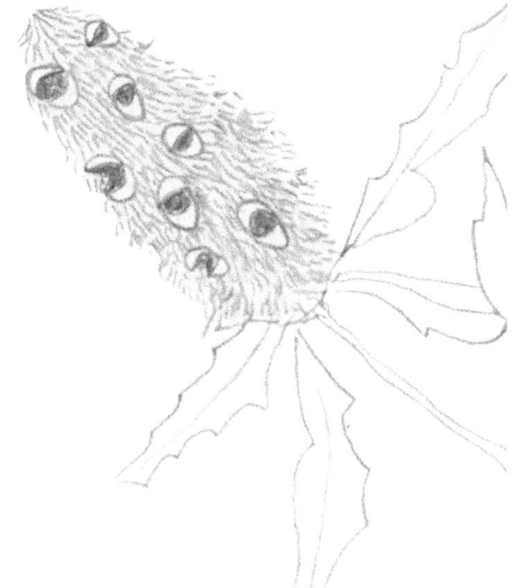

Journaling Prompts - Exploring Breath and Flow

Where do I hold tension or restriction in my body?

How does my breathing reflect my current emotional state?

What natural rhythms around me mirror my breath?

How can I use my breath to reconnect when I feel disconnected or overwhelmed?

Where do I hold my breath in life?

How does exhaling feel as an act of letting go?

What patterns am I ready to release through exhalation?

Practice 6 – Geometry of Belonging

Seeing patterns and symmetry as proof of connection

Nature is full of patterns, spirals in shells, branching in trees, hexagons in honeycombs. These forms are more than beauty; they are signs of order, connection, and life's intelligence. Observing natural geometry can help you feel aligned, grounded, and part of something larger.

For beginners, noticing patterns can be as simple as opening your eyes and observing. It's a way to slow down, engage your senses, and recognise the subtle structures that link all living things, including yourself.

Observing patterns helps you:

- Feel connected to the larger web of life.
- Recognise symmetry and imperfection in yourself and your surroundings.
- Develop mindfulness and focus.
- Inspire creativity and reflection.

In-Nature Practice - Observing Patterns

Notice repeating forms, symmetry, and natural designs.

- Walk or sit in a natural space. Look closely at leaves, shells, bark, spiderwebs, or water ripples.
- Identify repeating shapes, spirals, or arrangements. Don't worry about understanding them scientifically; just observe.
- Sketch or photograph patterns that capture your attention.
- Reflect on where you notice symmetry, imperfection, or unexpected order.

At-Home Practice - Drawing Your Own Patterns

Engage creatively with natural patterns and reflect on personal connections.

- Gather paper, pens, or pencils.
- Draw patterns inspired by your observations in nature. These could be mandalas, spirals, or geometric shapes.
- Focus on repetition, symmetry, and flow to allow your mind to relax.
- Journal about what these patterns feel like, or what they remind you of in your life.

Journaling Prompts - Exploring Patterns and Belonging

What patterns do I repeat that no longer serve me?

What shapes or forms symbolise balance to me?

Where in my life do I notice harmony and order?

How do imperfections reveal their own kind of beauty?

Where do I feel disconnected or out of alignment?

Which shapes or forms inspire calm, balance, or energy?

Practice 7 – The Language of Trees

Grounding, patience, and silent communication

Trees are among the oldest living beings on Earth. They teach patience, resilience, and groundedness. Their slow, steady growth reminds us that life unfolds in its own rhythm, and that connection to the Earth is a deep, ongoing process.

For someone new to nature journaling, spending time with a tree can be a simple yet profound practice. Trees offer a quiet companionship, encouraging you to slow down, notice seasonal changes, and reflect on your own growth.

Connecting with trees can help you:

- Feel grounded and centred.
- Develop patience and perspective.
- Recognise the slow, unfolding nature of personal growth.
- Experience a sense of silent companionship.

In-Nature Practice - Befriending a Tree

Observe, connect, and reflect on lessons from a single tree.

- Choose a tree to visit regularly in a park, garden, or nearby street.
- Sit quietly under or near the tree for 5–10 minutes. Notice:
  - The texture of bark.
  - The shape and movement of branches.
  - The roots (if visible.)
- Observe the tree over time. Look for changes in leaves, buds, or shadows.
- Journal your impressions, focusing on qualities the tree seems to express.

At-Home Practice - Tree-Inspired Reflection

Bring the tree's lessons into your indoor practice.

- Choose one tree you've connected with or imagine one in detail.
- Create art inspired by it: a drawing, poem, or letter.
- Brew tea or a warm drink and sit quietly, reflecting on the tree's qualities - patience, strength, flexibility. What else do you sense?
- Journal your insights, noting any connections to your own life.

Journaling Prompts - Listening to Trees

If I grew like a tree, what kind of forest would I create?

What am I ready to root into?

What qualities of the tree do I admire and wish to embody?

How does observing this tree change my sense of time?

Where am I reaching toward light or expansion?

Practice 8 – Water's Memory

Flow, emotional release, and adaptability

Water is a master of adaptability. It flows, moves around obstacles, and remembers the paths it has taken, yet it never clings. Observing water can teach us about emotional release, flexibility, and the art of going with the current.

For someone new to these practices, connecting with water can feel calming and grounding. Whether it's a river, rain, or even a bowl of water at home, water invites reflection and gentle self-awareness.

Engaging with water helps you:
- Release emotional tension and stress.
- Develop flexibility and resilience.
- Notice your own patterns of flow and resistance.
- Cultivate a sense of ease and connection with change.

In-Nature Practice - Observing Water

Learning from water's movement and flow.

- Find a body of water: a river, lake, ocean, or rainfall. If not possible, even a puddle or a fountain works.
- Sit or stand quietly and observe:
    - How the water moves around obstacles.
    - Patterns, ripples, or reflections.
    - Sounds and rhythms.
- Speak aloud one emotion or thought you wish to release, imagining it flowing away with the water.
- Journal your observations and reflections.

At-Home Practice - Water Ritual

Connect with water's cleansing and flowing qualities indoors.

- Use a bowl of water, a cup of tea, or a mindful shower.
- Pay attention to the sensation of water touching your skin or hands.
- Imagine that each drop carries away tension, worry, or unwanted energy.
- Afterwards, journal what shifted physically, mentally, or emotionally.

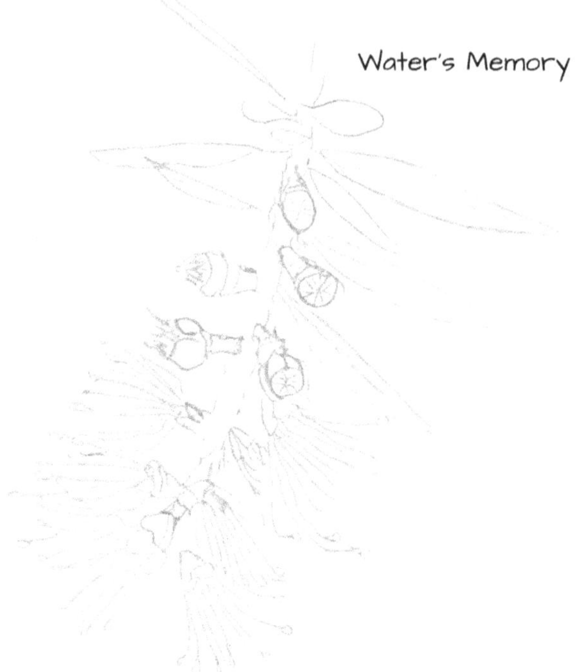

Journaling Prompts - Embracing Flow

What am I holding that wishes to move through me?

Where in my life can I be more fluid and adaptable?

How does water reflect my emotional state today?

What can I learn from water about patience and persistence?

How do I feel when I surrender to life's flow?

Practice 9 – Fire of Renewal

Transformation, passion, and courage

Fire is a symbol of transformation. It consumes and illuminates, teaching both surrender and vitality. Observing or interacting with fire can help us release what no longer serves us and ignite inner courage, creativity, and energy.

For beginners, fire can feel powerful or even intimidating. This practice invites you to approach fire safely, observe its qualities, and reflect on what it can teach about your own transformation and inner spark.

Connecting with fire helps you:

- Release old patterns or emotional baggage.
- Access courage and inner motivation.
- Observe the balance between letting go and embracing energy.
- Foster a sense of vitality and aliveness.

In-Nature Practice - Fire Observation

Witness transformation and energy through fire.

- Build a safe fire outdoors if possible, or observe a campfire, candle, or fireplace.
- Sit quietly and watch the flame. Notice:
  - Movement and shapes.
  - Heat and light.
  - Changes over time.
- Write one word, feeling, or intention you are ready to release and offer it to the flame (safely!)
- Journal your reflections afterwards.

At-Home Practice - Creative Fire Ritual

Engage with fire symbolically through daily life.

- Use a candle, stovetop, or oven safely. Even cooking can be symbolic of fire.
- Focus on the act as a transformation: ingredients change, wax melts, or flame illuminates.
- Reflect on what old patterns, thoughts, or habits you want to transform.
- Journal insights and feelings about courage, passion, or letting go.

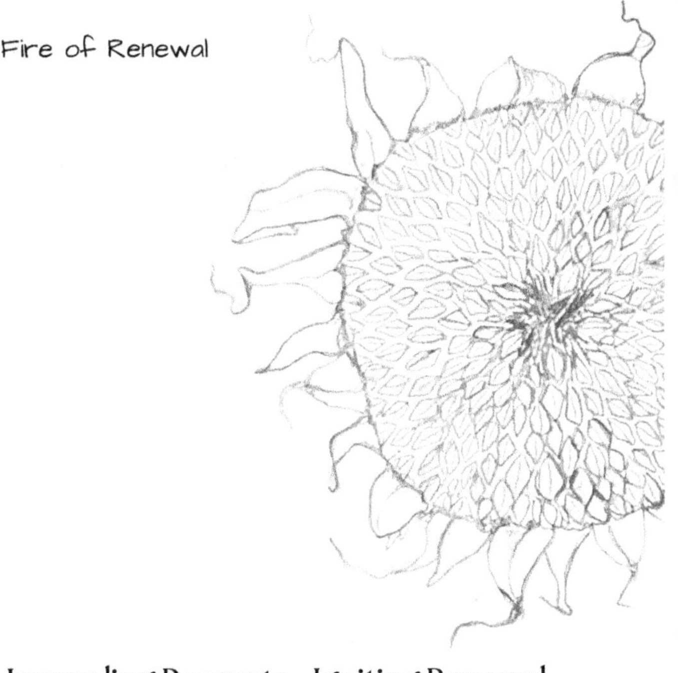

Journaling Prompts - Igniting Renewal

What needs to burn away to make space for new growth?

What ignites me most naturally?

Where in my life can I embrace transformation rather than resist it?

How can I cultivate courage and passion in small daily ways?

What sparks joy, courage, or energy in me?

Which passions have I neglected that could be reignited?

Practice 10 – Listening to the Sky

Air, spaciousness, and perspective

The sky is a vast, ever-changing presence above us. It teaches impermanence, spaciousness, and perspective. Clouds drift, stars move, and light shifts, yet the sky itself remains. Observing it can help you feel both grounded and expansive, offering a sense of calm and connection.

For beginners, looking at the sky can feel simple, yet profoundly grounding. By noticing its changes, you begin to develop awareness of cycles, space, and your own place within the larger world.

Engaging with the sky helps you:
- Cultivate spaciousness in mind and body.
- Notice impermanence and change without attachment.
- Expand perspective beyond immediate concerns.
- Feel a sense of connection to the natural world.

In-Nature Practice - Sky Observation

Connect with vastness and impermanence through the sky.

- Find an open outdoor space or a spot where you can see the sky clearly.
- Sit or stand quietly and observe:
    - Cloud shapes and movement.
    - Colours of the sky at different times of day.
    - Stars, moon, or planets at night.
- Reflect on your own thoughts and feelings as you observe the sky's vastness.
- Journal your impressions.

At-Home Practice - Indoor Sky Reflection

Bring the experience of spaciousness indoors.

- Open a window or use images of the sky to create a visual connection.
- Spend a few minutes noticing air movement, light, or imaginary clouds.
- Decorate a small space with symbols of the sky, e.g., a blue cloth, feather, or wind chime.
- Journal how observing or imagining the sky affects your mood, focus, or sense of space.

Journaling Prompts - Embracing Spaciousness

What thoughts drift like clouds through my awareness?

How can I create more inner space in my daily life?

When do I feel most expansive or restricted?

What lessons of impermanence and change can the sky teach me?

Where do I feel limited and need perspective?

What does openness feel like inside me?

Practice 11 – Human as a Bridge Between Worlds

The body as the living link of Earth and Sky

We are not separate from nature; we are nature becoming aware of itself. Our bodies connect the grounded Earth below and the vast sky above. By paying attention to our physical presence and energy, we can feel this connection more clearly.

For beginners, this practice encourages embodied awareness - noticing how your body interacts with the world, how energy flows through you, and how you are a living bridge between groundedness and expansiveness.

Recognising yourself as a bridge helps you:

- Feel integrated with the natural world.
- Develop balance between grounding and expansion.
- Increase awareness of your body and energy.
- Strengthen a sense of presence and belonging.

In-Nature Practice – Grounding and Expanding

Connect your body to both the Earth and the sky.

- Find an outdoor space where you can stand, sit, or lie down comfortably.
- Close your eyes and sense the Earth beneath you. Feel your weight, your roots connecting to the ground.
- Lift your awareness upward - sense the sky above, the air around you, and the space above your head.
- Imagine energy flowing from the Earth through your body and into the sky, and back again.
- Journal what you noticed about your body, energy, and sense of connection.

At-Home Practice - Body Awareness Scan

Cultivate embodied awareness indoors.

- Sit or lie down comfortably in a quiet space.
- Slowly scan your body from soles to crown, noticing sensations, tension, or ease.
- Imagine a connection from your feet to the Earth and from your head to the sky.
- Journal how this awareness shifts your sense of balance or energy.

Journaling Prompts - Connecting Body and World

When do I feel most at home in my body?

What does balance between grounding and expansion mean to me?

Where in my life do I notice disconnection between mind, body, and environment?

How can I honour my role as a bridge between inner and outer worlds?

Which energies flow easily through me, and which feel blocked?

Practice 12 – The Return to Coherence

Integration, gratitude, and ongoing practice

Reconnection is not a destination; it's a rhythm restored. After exploring breath, movement, natural elements, and cycles, this practice is about integrating those experiences into daily life. Coherence arises when your inner rhythms align with the natural world and your personal insights.

For beginners, this practice emphasises reflection and gentle integration, helping you notice shifts, gratitude, and ongoing ways to stay connected with yourself and nature.

Returning to coherence helps you:
- Recognise your own growth and transformation.
- Strengthen ongoing connections with nature and self.
- Develop practices to support balance, calm, and presence.
- Celebrate small achievements and insights along the journey.

<u>In-Nature Practice – Outdoor Gratitude Ceremony</u>

Integrate experiences and express gratitude for your connection with nature.

- Find a comfortable outdoor spot such as a garden, park, or balcony.
- Collect a small natural object (stone, leaf, feather) as a symbol of your journey.
- Spend a few minutes reflecting on your experiences, noticing how you've changed.
- Offer gratitude to the Earth, to yourself, and to the natural rhythms you've observed, silently or aloud.
- Journal your reflections and feelings after the ceremony.

<u>At-Home Practice - Letter to Your Future Self</u>

Consolidate learning and create a personal reminder of your coherence practice.

- Write a letter to yourself, that you will read one year from now. Include:
  - Insights you want to remember.
  - Daily practices or rituals that sustain connection.
  - Gratitude for your own growth.
- Seal the letter or place it somewhere safe.
- Optional: create a small daily ritual (lighting a candle, journaling, or mindful observation) to reinforce coherence.

Journaling Prompts - Sustaining Coherence

How has nature changed me?

What daily acts keep me aligned with the living field?

Which insights from my journey do I want to carry forward?

How can I continue to integrate presence and awareness into everyday life?

What daily rituals support my connection to life?

Practice 13 – Animal Allies

Connection, intuition, and guidance through the animal world

Animals can be teachers, guides, and mirrors of our inner selves. By observing their behaviour, presence, and patterns, we can gain insight into our own instincts, strengths, and areas for growth. Even urban wildlife or pets can offer lessons about attention, play, patience, and adaptability.

For beginners, connecting with animals is about noticing, respecting, and learning from their presence. It is a gentle way to deepen awareness and recognise the interconnectedness of life.

Observing animals helps you:

- Cultivate intuition and attentiveness.
- Recognise qualities you share with or wish to develop from animals.
- Strengthen your connection to the natural world.
- Learn patience, observation, and empathy.

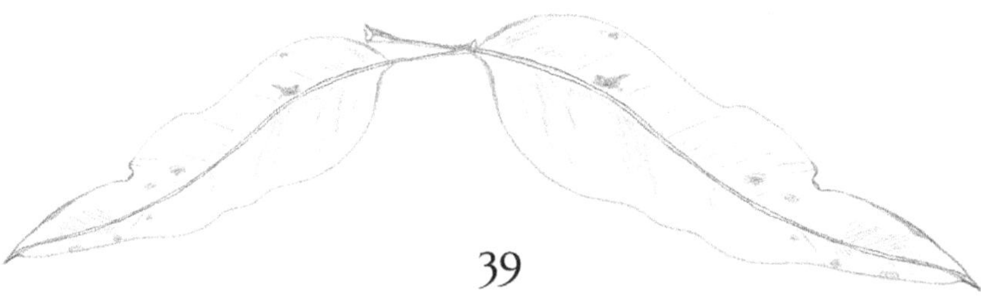

In-Nature Practice – Observing Animal Behaviour

Notice, learn, and reflect from animals around you.

- Visit a natural space, garden, or park where animals are present. If outside access is limited, observe birds, insects, or pets at home.
- Sit quietly and watch an animal for several minutes. Notice:
  - Movements and patterns.
  - Sounds and calls.
  - Interaction with the environment.
- Reflect on qualities the animal exhibits: curiosity, patience, focus, playfulness.
- Journal what you observe and what lessons might apply to your own life.

At-Home Practice - Animal-Inspired Reflection

Bring insights from animals into creative or contemplative practice.

- Choose an animal you feel drawn to or have observed recently.
- Create art, write a poem, or journal about the qualities it represents.
- Reflect on how these qualities appear or could appear in your life.
- Optional: keep a small "animal allies" notebook to record ongoing observations and lessons.

Journaling Prompts - Learning from Animal Allies

Which animal qualities resonate with me most right now?

What instincts or inner wisdom am I ignoring?

How can I practice presence like the animals I observe?

Which animal would I call as a guide or ally for this season of life?

Practice 14 – Edible Wisdom

Connection, nourishment, and mindful consumption

Food is not just fuel; it is a direct way to connect with the Earth. Plants, herbs, fruits, and vegetables carry the wisdom of the soil, sun, and rain. By paying attention to what we eat, how we prepare it, and where it comes from, we can develop a deeper awareness of the cycles of nature and our own relationship to nourishment.

For beginners, edible wisdom is about mindful observation and gratitude, noticing the life energy in food and how it interacts with your body and spirit.

Engaging with food mindfully helps you:

- Cultivate gratitude and awareness for the natural world.
- Recognise the connection between your choices and the Earth.
- Nourish your body and mind consciously.
- Discover insights about cycles, growth, and sustainability.

<u>In-Nature Practice – Foraging and Observation</u>

Learn from edible plants and observe natural abundance.

- Visit a garden, park, or safe wild space to notice edible plants, herbs, or fruit.
- Observe the plant carefully: notice the colours, shapes, textures, and smells.
- If safe and permitted, taste a small portion mindfully. Notice the flavour, texture, and energy it provides.
- Reflect on the plant's growth, environment, and what it teaches about nourishment and cycles.
- Journal your observations.

<u>At-Home Practice - Mindful Eating Ritual</u>

Deepen connection to food and your body through attention and reflection.

- Choose one meal or snack to eat slowly and mindfully.
- Before eating, take a moment to observe the colours, smells, and textures.
- As you eat, notice each bite's flavour, how it moves through your body, and the energy it provides.
- Reflect on your relationship with food. Where do you naturally display gratitude, awareness, and presence, or where can you intentionally add these?
- Journal your insights.

Journaling Prompts - Discovering Edible Wisdom

What does my body truly need right now?

How does mindful eating change my experience of food?

What lessons about growth and cycles can I learn from plants I consume?

How can I honour the life and energy of the food I eat?

Which foods, tastes, or textures bring me vitality?

What flavours in life do I crave and why?

Practice 15 – The Shadow of Wildness

Embracing untamed aspects of self and nature

Wildness is not only found in untamed forests, rivers, or creatures; it also lives within us. This practice explores the parts of yourself that resist structure, crave freedom, or feel hidden - your inner "wild self." By acknowledging and engaging with these shadows, you can discover untapped creativity, resilience, and authenticity.

For beginners, exploring wildness can feel unfamiliar or even uncomfortable. The key is gentle observation, curiosity, and reflection, noticing where you are constrained and where you can allow more freedom.

Connecting with your inner wildness helps you:
- Embrace authenticity and hidden potential.
- Release fear or limiting beliefs.
- Cultivate courage and creativity
- Recognise and integrate shadow aspects into a fuller self.

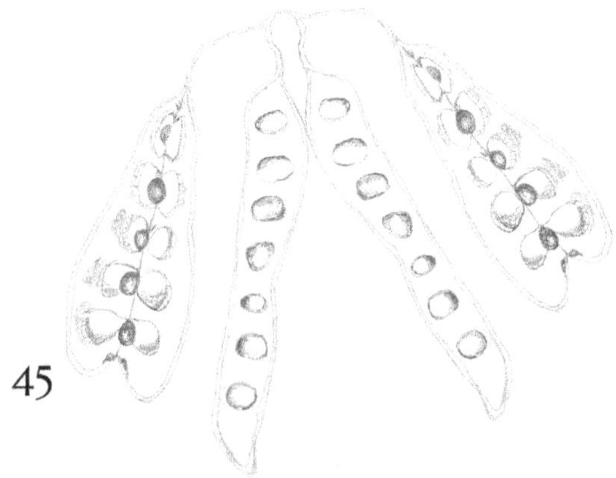

<u>In-Nature Practice – Meeting Your Wild Self</u>

Observe and reflect on untamed energy in nature and within yourself.

- Visit a natural area, such as a forest, riverbank, or open field.
- Spend a few minutes noticing untamed elements:
  - Twisting branches, moss, wind-swept leaves.
  - Animals moving freely.
  - Sounds of nature unbound by human order.
- Reflect on how these wild elements mirror aspects of your inner self.
- Journal freely, exploring both admiration and resistance to this wildness.

<u>At-Home Practice - Shadow Exploration</u>

Engage creatively with your untamed inner self.

- Choose a quiet space for reflection or creative expression.
- Use drawing, writing, or movement to explore your "wild side." Engage with untamed emotions, impulses, or desires.
- Observe without judgment; notice patterns, feelings, or insights.
- Journal about how these aspects could be integrated into your life constructively.

Journaling Prompts - Embracing Wildness

What parts of myself feel untamed or hidden?

Where do I resist freedom or spontaneity?

How can I honour my wildness in daily life?

What lessons can I learn from untamed elements in nature?

Which parts of me are waiting to be acknowledged?

What would it feel like to honour my inner wildness daily?

Practice 16 – Soundscapes

Listening deeply to the auditory world and inner resonance

Sound surrounds us constantly, from the rustle of leaves to the hum of a city. Nature's sounds (e.g., wind, water, birds, and insects) carry rhythm, mood, and subtle messages. Paying attention to sound can deepen presence, awaken intuition, and reveal connections between your inner state and the world around you.

For beginners, listening carefully may feel unusual at first, especially in a noisy or busy environment. The practice is about noticing patterns, tones, and rhythms and observing how they affect your mind, body, and emotions.

Engaging with sound helps you:
- Heighten awareness and mindfulness.
- Connect with natural rhythms and subtle energy.
- Recognise emotional patterns reflected in sound.
- Develop intuition and creative insight.

In-Nature Practice – Listening Walk

Explore natural soundscapes and your inner resonance.

- Go for a quiet walk in nature, a park, or even your backyard.
- Pause periodically and close your eyes. Notice:
  - Repeating patterns or rhythms (bird calls, rustling leaves, flowing water.)
  - Sounds you typically ignore.
  - How different sounds make you feel physically and emotionally.
- Optionally, hum, whisper, or make soft sounds in response to nature.
- Journal your observations, noting patterns, feelings, or insights.

At-Home Practice - Sound Awareness Practice

Bring mindful listening indoors.

- Sit quietly in a room or near a window.
- Focus on ambient sounds: distant traffic, a ticking clock, or wind outside.
- Notice which sounds feel harmonious and which create tension in your body or mind.
- Experiment with listening to music or natural sound recordings with full attention, observing your bodily and emotional reactions.
- Journal your reflections on what you noticed and how it influenced your awareness.

Journaling Prompts - Tuning into Sound

Which natural sounds bring me peace or clarity?

What sounds do I usually ignore, and what might they be telling me?

How do my emotions shift in response to different soundscapes?

What inner rhythms or tones can I discover by listening carefully?

How do I respond when my inner life feels noisy?

Which sounds make me feel alive, grounded, or joyful?

Practice 17 – The Edge of Mystery

Embracing uncertainty, curiosity, and wonder

Nature is full of mysteries, hidden trails, unexpected encounters, and subtle phenomena we may not fully understand. The edge of mystery invites us to lean into the unknown, cultivate curiosity, and embrace wonder. This practice encourages openness rather than control, allowing new insights, creativity, and self-discovery to emerge naturally.

For beginners, stepping into mystery may feel unfamiliar or even uncomfortable. The key is gentle exploration with curiosity, without pressure to "figure it out."

Exploring mystery helps you:
- Expand imagination and creative thinking.
- Become comfortable with uncertainty and change.
- Notice new perspectives or insights.
- Deepen trust in your intuition and the natural world.

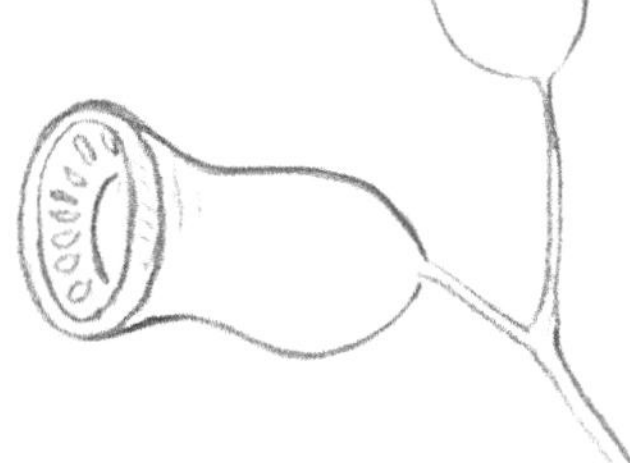

In-Nature Practice – Walking the Unknown

Engage with the unfamiliar and notice insights that arise.

- Visit a natural area you've not explored before: a new trail, park, or garden corner.
- Walk slowly and without a predetermined goal, noticing:
  - Unexpected sights, sounds, or textures.
  - Surprises in movement, patterns, or encounters.
  - Feelings that arise when you don't know what comes next.
- Pause and reflect on what curiosity or intuition surfaces.
- Journal your observations and emotions.

At-Home Practice - Mystery and Imagination

Foster curiosity and openness indoors.

- Choose a small, mysterious object: a shell, stone, feather, or unusual plant.
- Observe it closely: notice colours, shapes, textures, and patterns.
- Imagine its history, journey, or story in nature.
- Journal freely about your reflections, including feelings, stories, or questions that arise.

Journaling Prompts - Embracing the Unknown

Where in my life am I resisting the unknown?

What small mysteries can I explore today?

How does uncertainty feel in my body, and what can I learn from it?

What insights arise when I let go of the need to control outcomes?

What small wonders have I overlooked recently?

Practice 18 – Rituals of Reconnection

Creating intentional practices to deepen connection with self and nature

Rituals are simple, repeatable acts that signal attention, intention, and presence. In nature, rituals can help you mark transitions, honour cycles, and reinforce your connection to the world around you. Whether small daily actions or seasonal ceremonies, these practices bring rhythm, awareness, and meaning into life.

For beginners, rituals may feel unfamiliar or even ceremonial, which can be intimidating. The key is simplicity, intention, and personal meaning. Any action done mindfully can be a ritual.

Practising rituals helps you:
- Strengthen a sense of presence and alignment.
- Integrate nature's cycles into your life.
- Celebrate growth, release, and transformation.
- Foster connection with yourself, community, and the natural world.

In-Nature Practice – Simple Outdoor Ritual

Create a mindful practice to honour your connection with the Earth.

- Choose a natural spot: a garden, park, or nearby woodland.
- Decide on a simple ritual that feels meaningful, such as:
  - Offering a stone, leaf, or water to a tree or stream.
  - Lighting a small, safe candle outdoors.
  - Bowing or stretching in gratitude for the environment.
- Perform the ritual with attention and intention, noticing sensations, feelings, and thoughts.
- Journal your reflections afterwards, including insights or emotional shifts.

<u>At-Home Practice - Personal Reconnection Ritual</u>

Develop a mindful ritual that can be done indoors or at home.

- Identify a small, meaningful act that you can repeat daily or weekly, such as:
  - Lighting a candle and setting an intention.
  - Drinking tea slowly while reflecting on the day.
  - Journaling or drawing one thing you observed in nature.
- Perform the ritual with full attention, noticing physical sensations, emotions, and thoughts.
- Reflect on how the ritual shifts your sense of presence and connection.

Journaling Prompts - Designing Your Rituals

What small action can I do daily to honour my connection with nature?

Which times of day or week feel right for a personal ritual?

How do rituals shift my awareness or energy?

What intention or meaning do I want to embed in my rituals?

How can I create my own meaningful ceremonies?

Which rituals make me feel present and alive?

Which small acts keep me grounded?

Practice 19 – Night and Dream Work

Exploring darkness, dreams, and subconscious wisdom

Nighttime is a natural rhythm of rest, reflection, and introspection. Dreams are a doorway into the subconscious, offering guidance, insight, and creative inspiration. Engaging with night and dreams encourages self-awareness, intuition, and connection to cycles of rest and renewal.

For beginners, paying attention to dreams and the night may feel unfamiliar or abstract. The key is gentle observation, journaling, and curiosity, without pressure to "interpret perfectly."

Exploring night and dreams helps you:

- Connect with inner wisdom and intuition.
- Recognise patterns, symbols, and messages from the subconscious.
- Cultivate a sense of wonder and mystery.
- Integrate rest and reflection into your daily life.

In-Nature Practice – Night Observation

Deepen awareness of the nocturnal world.

- Find a safe outdoor space at night: your backyard, balcony, or local park.
- Sit or lie quietly, observing the night sky, moon, stars, and surrounding sounds.
- Notice subtle shifts in temperature, light, and sound.
- Reflect on how darkness feels in your body and mind.
- Journal your observations, impressions, and feelings.

At-Home Practice - Dream Journaling

Engage with dreams and subconscious messages.

- Keep a notebook by your bed.
- Upon waking, jot down any dreams or fragments of dreams, even single images or emotions.
- Reflect on recurring themes, symbols, or feelings.
- Explore what insights or questions arise from these dreams.

Journaling Prompts - Navigating Night and Dreams

What feelings or images appear most often in my dreams?

How does darkness or night affect my body, mind, and emotions?

What messages or guidance can I receive from my dreams?

How can I honour rest, reflection, and dream work in daily life?

What messages do my dreams bring me?

Which intuitive messages come when I rest?

Where in life am I ignoring my intuition?

Practice 20 – Star Gazing

Connecting with the vastness of the universe and our place within it

Looking up at the night sky can remind us of the vastness beyond ourselves, helping cultivate humility, wonder, and a sense of connection to something greater. Stars, planets, and cosmic patterns invite reflection on cycles, time, and our own life's rhythm.

For beginners, stargazing may feel overwhelming at first. The key is curiosity, presence, and gentle observation rather than scientific accuracy. The goal is to feel awe, wonder, and a sense of alignment with the cosmos.

Engaging with the cosmos helps you:
- Develop new perspectives on life's challenges and possibilities.
- Cultivate awe, curiosity, and creativity.
- Strengthen a sense of belonging in the larger web of life.
- Connect cycles of Earth with cycles of the universe.

<u>In-Nature Practice – Night Sky Observation</u>

Deepen awareness of cosmic patterns and personal reflection.

- Find a safe outdoor location with a clear view of the night sky.
- Sit quietly and allow your eyes to adjust to the darkness.
- Observe:
  - Stars, moon, planets, or constellations.
  - Movement of the sky over time.
  - Feelings and thoughts that arise when looking upward.
- Optionally, pick one star or constellation and quietly reflect on its symbolism or energy.
- Journal your observations, feelings, and any intuitive insights.

<u>At-Home Practice - Cosmic Reflection</u>

Integrate cosmic awareness into daily life, even indoors.

- If the night sky is not visible, use a star map, planetarium app, or online star chart.
- Focus on a single celestial body or pattern.
- Reflect on its qualities: endurance, distance, light, or movement.
- Journal about how these qualities relate to your life, challenges, or personal growth.

Journaling Prompts - Cosmic Awareness

What emotions or thoughts arise when I look at the night sky?

What sense of connection or belonging do I feel with the universe?

What lessons about patience, timing, or cycles can I learn from the cosmos?

How do I hold wonder in everyday life?

How can I expand my perspectives in daily life?

Which infinite possibilities excite or scare me?

What does the night sky reveal about my place in the world?

How does wonder shape my choices or actions?

Practice 21 – Connection with Soil

Grounding, cycles of life, and embracing transformation

Soil is the foundation of life. It nourishes plants, holds water, and supports ecosystems, while decay and decomposition return nutrients to the earth. By engaging with soil and the natural process of decay, we can develop a deeper sense of grounding, acceptance, and awareness of life's cycles.

For beginners, soil and decay may seem "messy" or unappealing. This practice is about noticing, respecting, and learning from these essential processes rather than avoiding them.

Connecting with soil and decay helps you:

- Feel physically and emotionally grounded.
- Understand life, death, and renewal as natural cycles.
- Cultivate patience, humility, and acceptance.
- Appreciate the unseen work that sustains life.

In-Nature Practice – Observing Soil and Decomposition

Deepen awareness of life's cycles through direct contact with the earth.

- Find a patch of soil in a garden, forest, or park.
- Sit or kneel quietly and observe:
  - Texture, colour, and moisture of the soil.
  - Signs of life: insects, roots, fungi, or decaying leaves.
- Touch the soil with your hands, noticing temperature and texture.
- Reflect on decay as part of renewal. Notice how old leaves, fallen branches, or dead plants nourish new growth.
- Journal your observations, feelings, and insights.

At-Home Practice - Soil Connection Ritual

Create a mindful practice using soil, compost, or plants.

- Bring soil or potted plants into your home or garden.
- Engage in mindful observation, touching, and tending to the soil.
- Reflect on:
  - What you are letting go of in your own life.
  - What you are nurturing or growing.
- Journal about how this ritual connects you to cycles of life and decay.

Journaling Prompts - Embracing Soil and Decay

How do I relate to the cycles of growth and decay in my own life?

What can I release to nourish my own growth?

How does touching or observing soil make me feel grounded?

What lessons about patience, transformation, or support can I learn from soil?

What aspects of myself are ready to decompose and transform?

Where can I ground myself more fully?

How do I feel about endings and beginnings?

Which cycles of renewal can I trust in my own life?

Practice 22 – Storytelling and Myth in Nature

Discovering meaning, connection, and wisdom through stories

Humans have always used stories and myths to make sense of the natural world and to explain the cycles of life, the behaviour of animals, and the forces of nature. Nature itself is full of narratives waiting to be noticed: the journey of a river, the life of a tree, the migration of birds.

For beginners, weaving stories around nature may feel imaginative or even unusual, but storytelling is a powerful tool to connect with meaning, remember lessons, and awaken creativity.

Engaging with storytelling and myth in nature helps you:
- See patterns, lessons, and connections in the natural world.
- Develop creativity, imagination, and reflection.
- Cultivate a deeper sense of belonging.
- Translate natural experiences into personal insight.

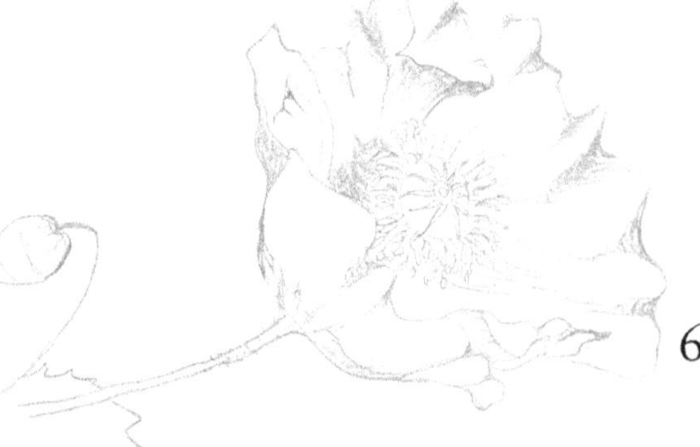

<u>In-Nature Practice – Nature Story Observation</u>

Create narratives inspired by natural surroundings.

- Sit in a natural space such as a park, forest, or garden.
- Observe carefully:
  - A tree, a rock, a river, or a plant.
  - The interactions of animals or elements.
- Imagine a story for what you observe:
  - How did it come to be?
  - What journey has it undertaken?
  - What lessons might it hold?
- Journal your story, feelings, and insights.

<u>At-Home Practice - Myth-Making Practice</u>

Engage with nature creatively through writing or art.

- Choose an element of nature you've observed recently.
- Invent a myth, legend, or personal story around it.
- Reflect on the lessons, symbols, or emotions that arise.
- Journal freely, exploring connections between the story and your own life.

Journaling Prompts - Storytelling and Myth

What story does this tree, river, or animal want to tell me?

How can I see my own life as a story connected to nature?

Which myths or legends resonate with the natural elements around me?

How can I use storytelling to deepen my awareness and connection?

Which myths hold me back, and which empower me?

How can I use imagination to understand myself?

Practice 23 – Sacred Waterways

Honouring rivers, streams, lakes, and the life they sustain

Waterways are lifelines of the Earth, carrying nourishment, life, and stories through the land. They have been regarded as sacred across cultures as places of reflection, healing, and transformation. Engaging with water encourages flow, adaptability, and reverence for life's currents.

For beginners, connecting with waterways may feel simple but deeply grounding. It's less about understanding and more about presence, listening, and noticing how water moves and affects you.

Connecting with waterways helps you:

- Cultivate adaptability and flow in your life.
- Deepen presence through sensory awareness.
- Recognise cycles of giving, receiving, and renewal.
- Foster gratitude and reverence for natural systems.

<u>In-Nature Practice – Observing a Waterway</u>

Deepen your connection to the movement and life of water.

- Find a natural water source such as a river, stream, pond, or even rainfall.
- Sit quietly nearby and observe:
  - Movement and patterns of the water.
  - Sounds, reflections, and interactions with surrounding life.
  - Feelings and thoughts that arise in response to the water.
- Optionally, place a small natural object in the water as a symbolic offering or intention.
- Journal your observations, emotions, and insights.

<u>At-Home Practice - Water Ritual</u>

Bring mindful connection to water into your daily life.

- Use a bowl of water, a cup of tea, or even a shower as your focus.
- Observe:
  - Temperature, movement, and sound.
  - Sensations in your body as you interact with it.
- Reflect on what you wish to release or invite into your life through this practice.
- Journal your reflections after the ritual.

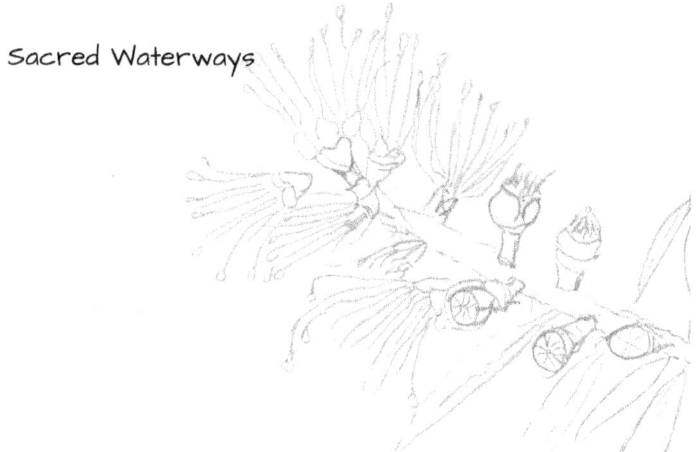

Journaling Prompts - Honouring Water

What does the flow of water teach me about my own life?

What emotional patterns could I release into the water?

How can I honour water as sacred in daily life?

Where do I need to release resistance?

How can I flow with life rather than against it?

Where do I feel stuck or blocked?

How can I allow life to flow more freely?

Which current in my life carries me toward growth?

Practice 24 – Wind as Messenger

Listening to air, movement, and subtle messages from nature

Wind is ever-present yet often unnoticed. It can carry seeds, sounds, scents, and even stories. By paying attention to the wind, you can develop sensitivity, awareness, and attunement to subtle energies. Wind invites curiosity, reflection, and a sense of connection to the wider world.

For beginners, noticing wind may feel abstract or simple, but subtle observation can reveal patterns, messages, and insights about your own inner state.

Connecting with wind helps you:
- Cultivate presence and sensory awareness.
- Develop intuition and receptivity to subtle signals.
- Recognise impermanence and movement in life.
- Feel connected to forces beyond the self.

In-Nature Practice – Listening to the Wind

Deepen awareness of movement, sound, and presence.

- Go to an open space or stand by a window where you can feel the breeze.
- Close your eyes and notice:
  - The direction, strength, and temperature of the wind.
  - Sounds it carries, such as rustling leaves, distant voices, or water.
  - Sensations on your skin and hair.
- Reflect on how the wind interacts with the environment and your body.
- Journal your observations, feelings, and any insights or messages that arise.

At-Home Practice - Wind Awareness Practice

Notice and honour the subtle presence of air indoors.

- Open a window or door to let air flow through your space.
- Sit quietly and focus on:
  - How the air moves across your skin.
  - Any changes in temperature or sound.
- Consider the "messages" the wind might carry insights, reminders, or inspiration.
- Journal reflections, sensations, and ideas that emerge.

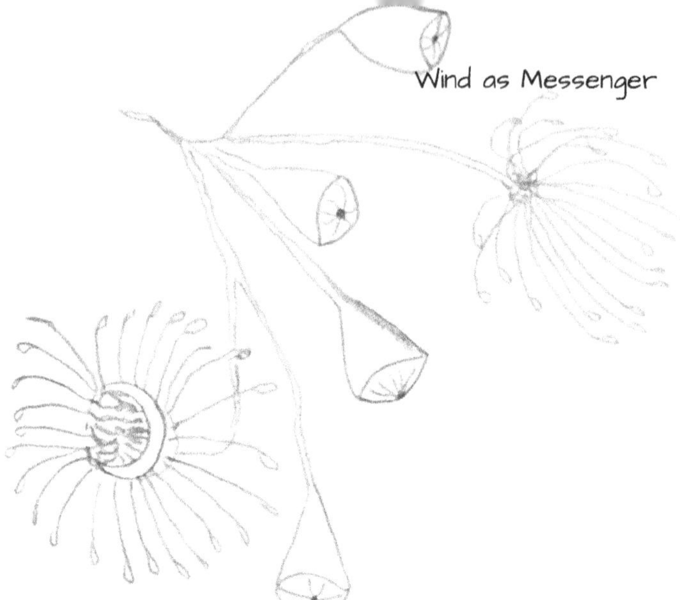

Journaling Prompts - Listening to the Wind

What emotions or thoughts arise as I notice the wind?

Where in my life could I allow more flow and flexibility?

What messages or insights might the wind be offering me?

How can I honour the presence of air and movement daily?

What am I holding too tightly?

What am I ready to release into the world?

Which messages come when I pause and listen?

How can I surrender control without fear?

Practice 25 – Wild Creativity

Awakening imagination, play, and self-expression through nature

Nature is inherently creative, from the intricate pattern of a spider's web to the colours of a sunset. By engaging with the natural world, you can awaken your own wild creativity, expressing thoughts, feelings, and ideas that might otherwise remain hidden.

For beginners, this may feel unusual or intimidating. The key is playfulness, curiosity, and letting go of judgment. Creativity is about exploration, not perfection.

Connecting with wild creativity helps you:

- Express yourself authentically.
- Build problem-solving and imaginative skills.
- Deepen connection with nature and your inner world.
- Experience joy, wonder, and flow.

In-Nature Practice – Creative Observation Walk

Inspire creative expression through sensory exploration.

- Take a walk in a natural area.
- Observe closely:
  - Colours, shapes, and textures.
  - Sounds, smells, and movement.
- Collect small natural objects (stones, leaves, feathers) that inspire you.
- Reflect on how these observations could inspire a story, poem, drawing, or movement.
- Journal or sketch your creative impressions.

At-Home Practice - Nature-Inspired Creative Practice

Translate your observations into creative expression.

- Choose a form of expression: drawing, writing, music, or movement.
- Use your nature observations or objects as inspiration.
- Focus on expression, not accuracy allowing playfulness and experimentation.
- Journal or reflect on how this creative act makes you feel.

Journaling Prompts - Awakening Wild Creativity

What aspects of nature inspire me to create?

Where in my life can I allow more play and experimentation?

How does creative expression connect me to my inner self?

What small acts of creativity can I incorporate into daily life?

Where in life do I feel creatively blocked?

Practice 26 - Thresholds and Boundaries

Honouring personal limits and the spaces between transitions

Thresholds mark transitions, stepping from one room to another, from day to night, or from one life phase to the next. Boundaries define safe and meaningful spaces, both physically and emotionally. Nature teaches us to recognise these edges and transitions, helping us move consciously and protect our energy.

For beginners, noticing thresholds and boundaries may feel elusive or subtle. The practice is about observing, respecting, and reflecting on the spaces between things rather than forcing change.

Connecting with thresholds and boundaries helps you:

- Recognise when to enter or step back.
- Protect emotional and physical energy.
- Appreciate transitions as natural and necessary.
- Foster mindfulness and self-awareness.

In-Nature Practice – Observing Natural Boundaries

Learn from edges, limits, and transitions in the environment.

- Find a natural edge: where forest meets grassland, shore meets water, or sun meets shadow.
- Observe carefully:
  - How different elements interact at the boundary.
  - How movement, growth, or change occurs there.
- Reflect on what these natural edges teach about transitions and limits in your life.
- Journal your observations, feelings, and insights.

At-Home Practice - Creating Personal Boundaries

Practice mindful attention to physical and emotional spaces.

- Identify a physical or personal boundary in your daily life (desk space, workspace, personal time).
- Mark or honour that boundary consciously, a small ritual, a sign, or simply awareness.
- Reflect on emotional boundaries: where you feel overstretched or safe.
- Journal your reflections on how boundaries affect your wellbeing and energy.

Journaling Prompts - Thresholds and Boundaries

What thresholds in my life feel significant right now?

Where do I need to create or reinforce boundaries?

How can I honour natural transitions in my body, emotions, and environment?

What can I learn from observing boundaries in nature?

Which transitions in life feel intimidating or inviting?

Where are my personal boundaries unclear?

Practice 27 – Time in Deep Nature

Immersing fully in the natural world to restore presence and perspective

Spending extended, uninterrupted time in nature allows you to slow down, observe deeply, and reconnect with your inner rhythm. Deep nature experiences help dissolve distractions, foster clarity, and reveal patterns often overlooked in daily life.

For beginners, this may feel unusual or challenging. The practice is about gradual immersion, patience, and mindful awareness, not hiking long distances or extreme outdoor adventures.

Time in deep nature helps you:
- Reduce mental clutter and stress
- Strengthen sensory awareness
- Experience a sense of belonging in the natural world
- Cultivate patience, reflection, and insight

<u>In-Nature Practice – Immersion Walk or Sit</u>

Experience unbroken presence in nature.

- Choose a quiet natural location: forest, beach, meadow, or park.
- Spend at least 30 minutes to an hour in one place, either sitting or walking slowly.
- Notice:
  - Sounds, smells, and textures.
  - Movements of animals, plants, or water.
  - Your own bodily sensations and breath.
- Avoid phones or distractions; allow the environment to guide your attention.
- Journal your observations, feelings, and any insights about your connection to nature.

<u>At-Home Practice - Nature Reflection Space</u>

Bring elements of deep nature into your daily environment.

- Create a small corner in your home with natural objects: stones, plants, shells, or wood.
- Spend 10–15 minutes observing, touching, or simply being with these objects.
- Reflect on sensations and insights, imagining the connection to the larger natural world.
- Journal about what this mini immersion teaches about presence, cycles, or patience.

Journaling Prompts - Experiencing Deep Nature

What sensations arise when I spend extended time in nature?

Where in life do I rush unnecessarily?

What rhythms of nature can I mirror in my day?

How does slowing down change my perspective on life or daily stress?

Which elements of nature draw my attention most, and why?

How can I integrate the calm and clarity of deep nature into daily life?

Practice 28 – Celebration of Senses

Awakening and appreciating the richness of sensory experience in nature

We often live in a "head-centred" way, focused on thoughts, plans, and tasks. Nature invites us to engage all our senses, reconnecting us to the present moment and the vibrant life around us. By celebrating sight, sound, touch, smell, and taste, we cultivate awareness, joy, and a deeper connection with ourselves and the world.

For beginners, this may feel unfamiliar, as many of us rarely pay full attention to sensory experiences. The key is curiosity, presence, and playful noticing rather than mastery or analysis.

Celebrating the senses helps you:

- Fully inhabit the present moment
- Strengthen perception and awareness
- Enhance appreciation and gratitude
- Connect more deeply to nature and your own body

In-Nature Practice – Sensory Exploration

Fully engage your senses outdoors.

- Find a quiet natural space: garden, park, forest, or beach.
- Take slow, deliberate steps or sit quietly and notice:
    - Sight: Colours, patterns, light, and shadows.
    - Sound: Birds, wind, water, insects, or distant noises.
    - Touch: Textures of leaves, bark, grass, or stones.
    - Smell: Earth, flowers, water, or rain.
    - Taste: If safe, a berry, herb, or just notice air flavours.
- Focus on one sense at a time for a few minutes, then rotate.
- Journal observations, sensations, and insights.

At-Home Practice - Sensory Mindfulness Practice

Bring sensory awareness into daily life indoors.

- Choose one sense to focus on at a time:
    - Sight: Observe a plant or natural object closely.
    - Sound: Listen to music or ambient nature sounds.
    - Touch: Feel textures of fabrics, stones, or objects.
    - Smell: Use herbs, essential oils, or flowers.
    - Taste: Eat mindfully, noticing flavours, textures, and aromas.
- Take 5–10 minutes for focused attention on each sense.
- Journal reflections, sensations, and insights.

Journaling Prompts - Awakening the Senses

Which sense do I most often ignore, and how can I bring it into awareness?

What feelings arise when I fully engage one sense at a time?

How can I use sensory awareness to deepen connection with nature?

What new insights or joys emerge when I celebrate my senses?

How can I engage more fully with the present?

What sensations bring me joy or grounding?

Practice 29 – Ceremony of the Self

Honouring your journey, presence, and connection with nature

A personal ceremony is a way to acknowledge growth, express gratitude, and integrate your experiences. Nature provides the perfect setting for ritual, offering symbols, materials, and inspiration. A ceremony doesn't need to be elaborate, it can be simple, heartfelt, and deeply meaningful.

For beginners, creating a personal ceremony may feel unfamiliar or intimidating. The focus is on intention, presence, and self-expression, not perfection or formality.

A ceremony of the self helps you:
- Celebrate your personal growth and connection with nature
- Reflect on experiences, lessons, and transformations
- Deepen awareness of inner and outer rhythms
- Strengthen a sense of belonging and self-respect

<u>In-Nature Practice – Creating Your Ceremony</u>

Honour yourself and your connection with the natural world.

- Choose a quiet, natural space where you feel safe.
- Gather small natural objects that resonate stones, leaves, flowers, or water.
- Set an intention for your ceremony, gratitude, release, renewal, or reflection.
- Engage in simple ritual actions:
  - Place objects in a meaningful arrangement.
  - Speak your intention aloud.
  - Offer a small gesture of release or appreciation (placing a stone, sprinkling water, etc.)
- Sit or move mindfully, absorbing the moment.
- Journal reflections, insights, and feelings after the ceremony.

<u>At-Home Practice - Mini Ceremony</u>

Bring ritual and reflection into your daily routine.

- Choose a small corner in your home for reflection.
- Gather objects, symbols, or reminders of your connection with nature.
- Set an intention: release, gratitude, or self-honour.
- Spend a few minutes in mindful observation, journaling, or meditation.
- Optional: mark the moment with a small gesture (lighting a candle or incense.)

Journaling Prompts - Ceremony of the Self

What do I wish to honour or acknowledge about myself today?

Which intentions or practices do I want to carry forward?

What can I release in this moment to create space for growth?

How does creating a ceremony connect me to nature and my inner self?

How can I celebrate my own resilience and creativity?

Practice 30 – The Living Air

Awareness of air as a vital element, sensation, movement, and personal preference

Air surrounds us constantly, yet most of us rarely notice it. It is essential for survival, carrying oxygen to our bodies, and influencing our mood, energy, and wellbeing. Indoor air can accumulate dust, odours, moisture, and pollutants, while outdoor air offers freshness, movement, and life.

This practice invites you to slow down and tune into the air around you. By noticing temperature, movement, and personal preferences, you begin to understand how this invisible element affects your body, mind, and connection to the natural world.

- Cultivating awareness of air improves presence and sensory perception.
- Understanding your preferences for warmth, breeze, or stillness can enhance comfort and wellbeing.
- Connecting with air outdoors fosters a subtle but powerful sense of freedom and vitality.

In-Nature Practice – Feeling the Air

Deepen awareness of air as a living, moving presence.

- Step outside and pause. Close your eyes if you like.
- Notice the air on your skin: is it warm or cool? Still or moving?
- Observe how your body responds: does it feel relaxed, energised, or alert?
- Explore different locations: shaded v sunny, open field v under trees, coastal breeze v calm interior.
- Journal your observations.

At-Home Practice - Air Awareness Indoors

Compare and improve indoor air quality while noticing personal comfort.

- Open a window or step onto a balcony. Take a few slow breaths, feeling the difference from indoor air.
- Notice scents, temperature, and movement indoors. Are there areas that feel stuffy, damp, or heavy?
- Move around or adjust ventilation to experiment with what feels best.
- Journal reflections and preferences.

Journaling Prompts - Connecting with Air

How does the movement of air affect my mood and energy?

Do I prefer warm, cool, still, or breezy air? Why?

When do I notice air the most in my day?

How can I invite fresher, moving air into my life and environment?

Describe a moment when air felt like a living presence around you.

Practice 31 – Breath Awareness

Mindful breathing for grounding, calm, and presence

Breath is the bridge between body, mind, and the natural world. We often breathe shallowly or unconsciously, missing the opportunity to use breath as a tool for calm, focus, and presence. Mindful breathing allows you to slow your internal pace, release tension, and become fully present in the moment.

Even just a few minutes of conscious breathing can:

- Reduce stress and anxiety
- Increase clarity and focus
- Deepen connection to your body and surroundings
- Foster a sense of calm, resilience, and well-being

In-Nature Practice – Mindful Breath Practice

Connect to your body, mind, and environment through conscious breathing

- Find a quiet spot outdoors. Sit or stand comfortably.
- Close your eyes and notice your natural breath without changing it.
- Try one or more of these techniques:
  - Flower Breath: Inhale slowly through your nose imagining smelling a flower; exhale gently through your mouth, releasing tension.
  - Hissing Exhale: Inhale through your nose long and deep; exhale through your mouth with a soft hissing sound, slowing your internal rhythm.
  - Box Breathing: Inhale through the nose for a count of 4, hold for 2, exhale for 4, hold for 2. Repeat several times.
  - Belly Breath: Place your hands on your belly; breathe in so your belly expands, then slowly exhale, feeling the hands lower. Repeat 5 times.
- Pay attention to sensations: the temperature, smell, and movement of the air. Notice how your body responds.

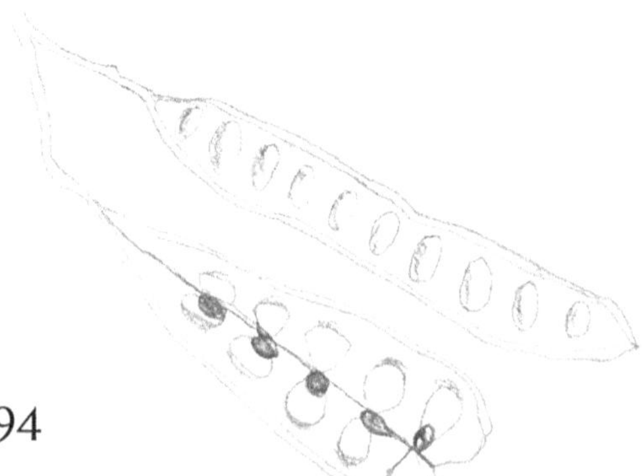

At-Home Practice - Affirmation Breath

Reinforce mindfulness and self-connection with breath and words

- Sit comfortably, close your eyes, and take slow, deep breaths.
- While inhaling and exhaling, silently repeat the following, emphasising the bolded word:
  - **THIS** breath is for me.
  - This **BREATH** is for me.
  - This breath **IS** for me.
  - This breath is **FOR** me.
  - This breath is for **ME.**
- Repeat for several cycles, noticing the calming and grounding effect.

Journaling Prompts - Exploring Breath

How does the movement of air affect my mood and energy?

Do I prefer warm, cool, still, or breezy air? Why?

When do I notice air the most in my day?

How can I invite fresher, moving air into my life and environment?

Describe a moment when air felt like a living presence around you?

Practice 32 – Clouds & Imagination

Observing the sky to inspire creativity, presence, and reflection

Clouds float freely across the sky, constantly changing shape and form. Observing them encourages curiosity, imagination, and mindfulness. This practice invites you to slow down, notice patterns, and allow your mind to wander in a calm, creative way.

Cloud-watching can help you:

- Reduce stress and mental chatter.
- Strengthen your connection to the natural world.
- Inspire creativity and playfulness.
- Notice subtle details in your environment, like birds, plants, and other wildlife.

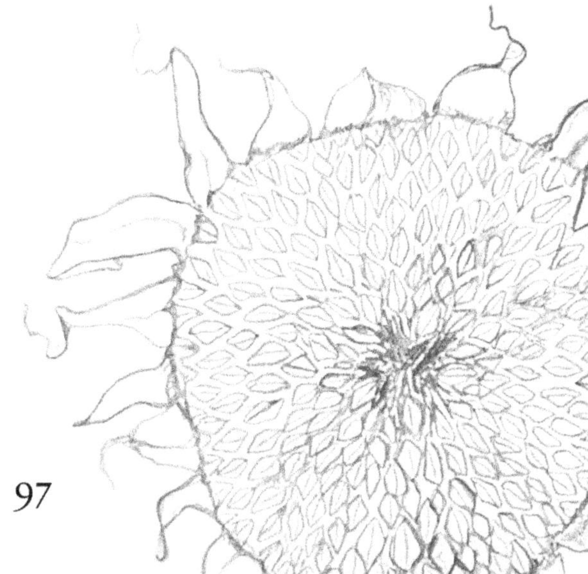

In-Nature Practice – Cloud Spotting

Connect with nature and imagination through mindful observation of clouds.

- Find a comfortable spot outdoors or near a window with a clear view of the sky.
- Observe the clouds without rushing. Notice shapes, colours, and movement.
- Use your imagination, what forms can you see? Animals, objects, abstract shapes?
- Sketch or note down the shapes you see in your journal. Don't worry about skill focus on expression and observation.
- Look beyond the clouds: notice birds, trees, or other elements in your environment.

At-Home Practice - Creative Reflection

Use cloud observation as inspiration for journaling or artwork.

- Sit near a window or step onto a balcony. Observe the sky and clouds.
- Sketch or write freely about the shapes you see. Don't censor your imagination.
- Reflect on whether the shapes feel random or hold personal meaning.
- Use this as a starting point for creative writing, poetry, or visual art.

Journaling Prompts - Exploring Clouds

Which cloud shapes caught my attention today? Why?

Do any clouds reflect feelings, thoughts, or memories I'm experiencing?

What do I notice about my surroundings while watching the clouds?

How does focusing on clouds change my mood or mindset?

Can I use cloud shapes as a metaphor for my own life or creative ideas?

Practice 33 – Dream Journaling

Using dreams as mirrors for self-awareness, insight, and reflection

Dreams are windows into the subconscious mind. They can reflect your emotions, hopes, fears, and sometimes even foresight. While they may seem strange or surreal, paying attention to your dreams can reveal patterns, recurring themes, and hidden wisdom about your waking life.

Dream journaling can help you:
- Gain insight into emotions, stress, and life challenges.
- Recognise recurring patterns or symbols in your life.
- Explore creativity and imagination.
- Strengthen your connection with your inner guidance.

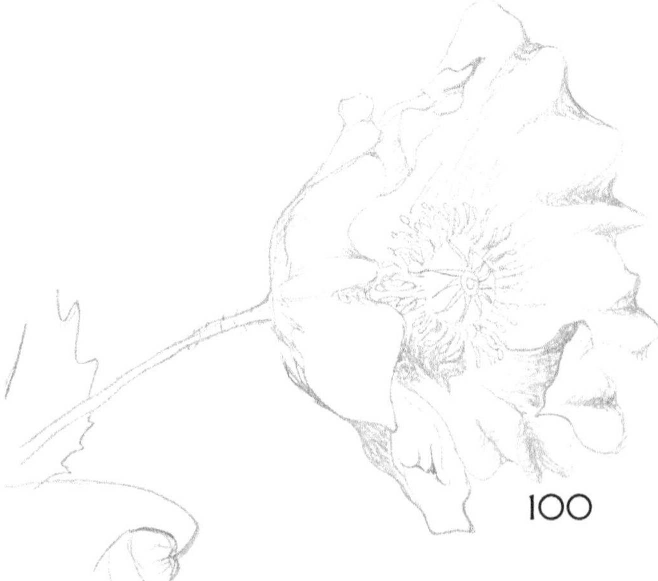

<u>In-Nature Practice – Dream Reflection Outdoors</u>

Connect your dream observations with the natural world for inspiration

- Find a quiet outdoor spot in the morning or evening.
- Reflect on your most recent dream. Close your eyes and visualise it as vividly as possible.
- Notice symbols, colours, or movements in the dream. Consider how they relate to your life, emotions, or surroundings.
- Write or sketch your dream in your journal, allowing images, feelings, and details to flow freely.

<u>At-Home Practice - Dream Journaling Practice</u>

Build a consistent habit of recording and reflecting on dreams

- Keep a journal and pen by your bedside.
- Upon waking, write down any dreams, even fragments, feelings, or strange images.
- Note recurring themes, symbols, or emotions over days and weeks.
- Reflect on patterns and connections to waking life: challenges, joys, anxieties, or inspirations.
- Optional: Use coloured pens, sketches, or symbols to make your dream journal visual and expressive.

Journaling Prompts - Exploring Your Dreams

What recurring symbols, people, or places appear in my dreams?

How do my dreams reflect challenges, emotions, or changes in my life?

Have I ever dreamed about something before it happened in real life? What might that mean?

Which dreams feel most vivid or significant, and why?

What can I learn about myself from paying attention to my dreams?

How might I use dream imagery in creative writing, art, or reflection?

Practice 34 – Feather: Messages from the Wild

Mindful wandering, sensory awareness, and noticing subtle signs in nature

Feathers are delicate, light, and often overlooked but they can be powerful reminders of presence, attention, and connection. Finding a feather on your path invites you to pause, observe, and connect fully with your surroundings. This Practice is about slow walking, mindful awareness, and using small signs in nature to guide reflection and grounding.

Feathers as a practice can help you:

- Slow down and immerse yourself in the present.
- Engage all your senses in observation.
- Foster mindfulness through gentle prompts in the natural world.
- Use small symbols as reminders for reflection and gratitude.

<u>In-Nature Practice – Feather Walk</u>

Connect deeply with the present moment through slow, mindful wandering

- Choose a natural space for a walk: park, garden, or woodland path.
- Begin with a few minutes of mindful breathing. Close your eyes if you like, noticing your inhale and exhale.
- Walk slowly, focusing on sensory experiences:
  - Feel the ground beneath your feet.
  - Notice the air on your skin.
  - Observe light, colour, movement, and patterns around you.
  - Smell the scents in your environment.
- Look for a feather along your path. If you find one, pick it up gently and bring it home.
- Add the feather to your journal. Write about:
  - How you felt before the walk.
  - How you felt during the walk.
  - How you feel after the walk.

At-Home Practice - Feather as Reminder

Use the feather as a mindfulness cue in everyday life

- Place your found feather in your journal, on a windowsill, or a small altar.
- Whenever you see it, pause and take a few mindful breaths.
- Reflect on how your senses and attention shift when you focus for a moment.
- Journal about the experience and any insights, feelings, or inspiration it brings.

Journaling Prompts - Feather as Guide

How does slowing down change the way I notice the world?

What senses do I usually overlook, and how can I engage them more?

How do small signs from nature, like a feather, shift my awareness or mood?

What feelings arise when I intentionally focus on the present moment?

How can I bring this sense of mindful wandering into my daily life?

Practice 35 – Grateful

Cultivating awareness and appreciation for the gifts in your life

Gratitude is a simple yet powerful practice that shifts your focus from what's missing to what is present and meaningful. It helps cultivate contentment, joy, and connection to yourself, others, and the natural world.

Spending time in nature can amplify gratitude. The feel of soil under your feet, the warmth of sunlight, or the sound of birds can awaken awareness of life's small but profound gifts. Gratitude is not just a feeling, it's a way of being and noticing the abundance around you.

Gratitude can help you:
- Notice and appreciate everyday blessings.
- Strengthen relationships and connection.
- Reduce stress and foster well-being.
- Cultivate a positive mindset and openness to life.

In-Nature Practice – Gratitude Walk

Engage with nature and your senses to awaken gratitude.

- Stand barefoot or with shoes off on the ground. Feel the earth beneath your feet. Notice texture, temperature, moisture, and weight.
- Walk slowly through a natural space. Engage your senses: notice sights, sounds, smells, and textures.
- Pause to reflect on things you feel grateful for in that moment: nature's beauty, the breeze on your skin, the sun's warmth.
- Collect a small natural object (leaf, stone, feather) to serve as a reminder of this gratitude.
- Journal your observations, feelings, and insights.

At-Home Practice - Gratitude Reflection

Build a consistent habit of noticing and appreciating blessings.

- Set aside a few minutes daily. Sit comfortably and breathe deeply.
- Reflect on:
  - People who support or inspire you.
  - Experiences or challenges you've overcome.
  - Small joys, comforts, or pleasures.
  - Beauty in nature around you.
- Write freely in your journal. Be open, non-judgmental, and descriptive.

Journaling Prompts - Cultivating Gratitude

Who has helped me recently, and how can I show my gratitude?

What small daily moments bring me joy or comfort?

What aspects of nature make me feel thankful or alive?

What challenges have I overcome that I can now appreciate?

How can I integrate gratitude into my daily routines?

How does practicing gratitude change my perspective on life?

Practice 36 – Listening: The Art of Awareness

Cultivating deep listening to your environment, self, and others

Listening is more than hearing, it's a conscious effort to notice, understand, and connect. In a world full of distractions and noise, slowing down to truly listen is a radical act. Nature offers an ideal space to practice this skill, helping you to sharpen attention, increase presence, and deepen connection with yourself and the world around you.

Mindful listening can help you:
- Strengthen focus and awareness.
- Notice subtle patterns and details in your environment.
- Improve communication and empathy with others.
- Cultivate calm, curiosity, and presence.

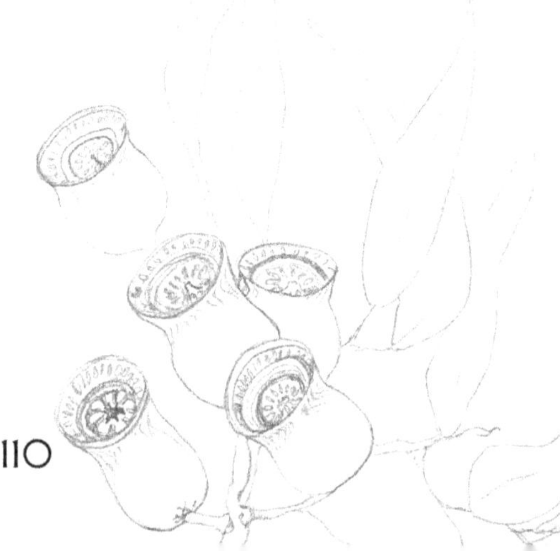

<u>In-Nature Practice – Expanding Your Hearing</u>

Notice and differentiate the layers of sound in your environment.

- Find a quiet spot outdoors. Sit comfortably and close your eyes.
- Take a few deep breaths to ground yourself.
- Begin by noticing the closest sounds: the feel of your own breath, rustle of clothing, or heartbeat.
- Gradually widen your awareness to include:
  - Nearby sounds (birds, insects, wind in trees.)
  - Mid-range sounds (footsteps, vehicles, distant voices.)
  - Far sounds (planes, distant traffic, weather changes.)
- Note which sounds are natural and which are man-made.
- Journal your observations, including what surprised you or brought awareness to a new aspect of your environment.

<u>At-Home Practice - Listening in Daily Life</u>

Practice mindful listening indoors or in your neighbourhood.

- Sit in a comfortable space and close your eyes.
- Observe all the sounds in your immediate environment: your body, home, and neighbourhood.
- Stretch your awareness gradually, noticing layers of sound at varying distances.
- Identify as many distinct sounds as you can and categorise them as natural or man-made.
- Journal reflections, focusing on what you noticed, your reactions, and any patterns.

Journaling Prompts - Deepening Listening

Which sounds do I usually overlook, and how does noticing them shift my awareness?

How does listening to nature compare to listening in urban or indoor spaces?

Which sounds make me feel calm, curious, or energised?

How can practicing listening improve my connection with myself and others?

Where can I find quiet or natural spaces to listen more deeply?

What patterns or rhythms in sound do I notice that mirror my inner life?

Practice 37 – Meditate: Presence in Nature

Cultivating focused awareness and presence through meditation

Meditation is the practice of bringing your attention back to the present moment, again and again, noticing sensations, thoughts, and the environment without judgment. It is not about "stopping thoughts," but about observing them and gently returning to the breath and body.

Nature provides an ideal setting for meditation, offering sounds, textures, and rhythms that support awareness and grounding. Practicing meditation outdoors strengthens your connection with your body, mind, and environment, reducing stress and cultivating clarity.

Benefits of meditation in nature include:

- Greater calm and stress reduction.
- Enhanced sensory awareness.
- Strengthened connection with yourself and the world around you.
- Increased presence, focus, and mental clarity.

In-Nature Practice – Grounded Meditation

Focus attention on body, breath, and surroundings.

- Find a quiet, comfortable spot outdoors: grass, sand, or a bench.
- Sit comfortably and close your eyes. Take a slow, deep breath.
- Notice the air entering through your nose, filling your lungs, and exhaling slowly.
- Relax your body and feel external sensations: sunlight, breeze, or the temperature of the ground beneath your feet.
- Expand awareness to your entire body in space. Feel your presence in the environment.
- Shift attention to sounds around you: birds, insects, wind through trees. Listen more deeply than usual.
- When ready, slowly open your eyes and focus on something beautiful. Allow your attention to expand, taking in the full scene with open awareness.
- Journal about your experience, sensations, and any insights that arose.

At-Home Practice - Indoor Meditation

Practice meditation using body, breath, and environmental awareness indoors.

- Sit comfortably in a quiet space with minimal distractions.
- Close your eyes and take slow, deep breaths.
- Feel your feet connecting to the floor and notice your body's contact with the chair or cushion.
- Observe ambient sounds in the room, outside, or far away.
- Open your eyes and focus on an object you find calming or beautiful, a plant, a piece of art, or a window view.
- Journal your sensations, feelings, and reflections.

Journaling Prompts - Deepening Meditation

What sensations in my body do I notice most when I meditate?

Which natural elements help me feel more grounded or present?

How does focusing on breath and environment shift my awareness?

What thoughts arise, and how can I observe them without judgment?

How does meditation affect my mood, stress levels, and sense of connection?

Can I notice subtle details in my surroundings that I normally overlook?

Practice 38 – Nature and Storytelling

Connecting to nature through narrative, myth, and personal reflection

Stories are a powerful way to understand the world and ourselves. Nature has inspired storytelling for millennia, from myths explaining the stars to tales of forests, rivers, and animals. By observing nature and reflecting creatively, you can craft your own stories, deepen your connection to the world, and explore your inner landscape.

Nature-inspired storytelling helps you:
- Develop creativity and imagination.
- Explore emotions and personal growth.
- Connect with cultural myths and ancestral wisdom.
- Strengthen your relationship with the natural world.

<u>In-Nature Practice – Observing and Imagining</u>

Use natural elements as prompts for storytelling.

- Find a natural space: forest, garden, beach, or park.
- Observe a plant, animal, rock formation, or natural pattern that draws your attention.
- Ask yourself questions:
  - "If this tree/rock/river could speak, what story would it tell?"
  - "What role might I play in this scene?"
  - "What emotions or lessons arise from this observation?"
- Write a short story, poem, or reflection inspired by the element. Focus on imagination, symbolism, or personal insight.

<u>At-Home Practice - Nature-Inspired writing</u>

Connect with natural themes through creative writing indoors.

- Gather natural objects (stones, shells, leaves) or photos of landscapes.
- Select one to focus on as your writing prompt.
- Write a narrative inspired by the object, considering:
  - What life might exist in or around it?
  - How does it change through seasons or weather?
  - What lessons could it teach?
- Reflect on any personal insights, metaphors, or emotions that emerge.

Journaling Prompts - Nature and Storytelling

What stories does nature inspire in me today?

Which animals, plants, or natural patterns hold symbolic meaning for me?

What lessons or insights emerge when I give voice to a tree, stone, or river?

How does imagining narratives in nature help me process my emotions?

Are there personal experiences I can reinterpret through a nature-inspired story?

What myths or folklore connect to the natural world around me?

Practice 39 – Your Nature Connection Place

Cultivating ongoing connection with a familiar place in nature

A sit spot is a special place in nature where you can go regularly to observe, reflect, and connect. It doesn't need to be grand or remote: a garden corner, a park bench, a quiet patch of forest, or even a balcony overlooking trees can serve as your sit spot.

By returning to the same place repeatedly, you begin to notice subtle rhythms of the natural world, the daily cycles, seasonal shifts, life cycles of plants and animals, and patterns in weather. Over time, this repeated practice fosters a sense of belonging, deepens awareness, and strengthens your connection with the living ecosystem.

Benefits of a sit spot practice include:
- Increased mindfulness and presence
- Deeper understanding of local nature patterns
- A sense of calm and grounding
- Connection with seasonal and daily cycles

In-Nature Practice – Establishing Your Sit Spot

Develop a personal, recurring connection with a single natural location.

- Choose a place you can visit regularly, preferably daily or weekly.

- Sit comfortably on the ground, a cushion, or a bench.

- Close your eyes or soften your gaze. Take a few deep breaths, grounding yourself.

- Observe your surroundings through all senses:

  - Sight: Colours, shapes, movement.

  - Sound: Birds, wind, water, distant noises.

  - Smell: Flowers, earth, leaves.

  - Touch: Air on skin, ground texture, temperature.

- Spend 10–20 minutes observing without an agenda. Simply notice what appears, changes, or remains constant.

- Journal observations, patterns, and feelings. Over time, reflect on changes across days, weeks, or seasons.

At-Home Practice - Sit Spot Visualisation

Bring the benefits of a sit spot indoors or when you can't go outside.

- Close your eyes and visualise your favourite natural sit spot.
- Imagine yourself sitting there comfortably, breathing deeply, and noticing the sights, sounds, and smells.
- Pay attention to subtle changes: light, movement, temperature, or sounds.
- Journal your experience, noting what you observed, how it made you feel, and any insights gained.

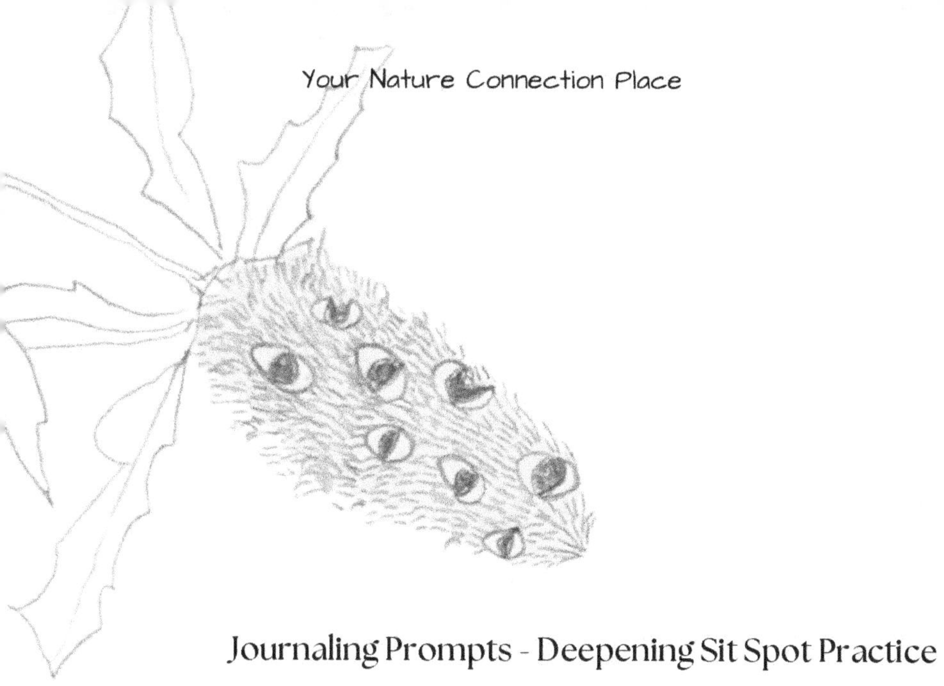

Journaling Prompts - Deepening Sit Spot Practice

What patterns or changes do I notice over repeated visits?

Which aspects of this spot feel comforting, grounding, or inspiring?

How does returning to the same place affect my awareness of daily or seasonal rhythms?

What small details have I never noticed before?

How can this practice help me feel more connected to the larger ecosystem?

What lessons about patience, observation, or change does my sit spot offer?

Practice 40 – Undistracted Mind

Cultivating focused attention to fully engage with the natural world

In our modern lives, distractions are constant: phones, screens, notifications, and endless to-do lists compete for our attention. This scattered focus can make it difficult to truly see, hear, and feel the world around us.

Nature offers a perfect environment to practice undistracted awareness. Even a few minutes of fully present observation allows your mind to settle, curiosity to flourish, and connection with the environment to deepen.

Practicing an undistracted mind helps you:
- Enhance curiosity and observation skills.
- Deepen connection with plants, animals, and ecosystems.
- Reduce stress and mental chatter.
- Increase presence, patience, and attentiveness.

In-Nature Practice – Focused Observation

Train attention and sensory awareness in a natural setting.

- Choose a quiet natural spot: a garden, park, forest path, or backyard.
- Leave electronic devices behind or in silent mode.
- Sit or stand comfortably and take a few deep breaths to ground yourself.
- Pick one focal point in nature: a tree, bird, flower, or patch of earth.
- Observe it for 5–10 minutes without distraction. Notice:
  - Movement: How leaves sway, water flows, or insects crawl.
  - Patterns: Shapes, colours, textures, and harmony.
  - Sounds: Birds, wind, rustling leaves, or distant sounds.
- Journal your observations and reflect on your ability to remain focused.

<u>At-Home Practice - Undistracted Nature Practice</u>

Bring focused attention into indoor or nearby natural settings

- Open a window or step into a garden or balcony.

- Choose one natural element to observe: a leaf, plant, flower, or cloud.

- Close your eyes briefly, then open them and focus all attention on the element.

- Notice details like colour, texture, light, shadows, and movement.

- Journal what you observed, how it felt to focus without distraction, and any insights.

Journaling Prompts - Cultivating an Undistracted Mind

Which distractions pull me away from observing nature most often?

What sensations or details do I notice when I am fully present?

How does being undistracted affect my curiosity and attention?

What can I learn from practicing focused observation in nature?

How can I create small moments of undistracted awareness daily?

What patterns or movements in nature emerge only when I give my full attention?

Practice 41 – Nature Rituals

Creating simple, mindful practices to deepen connection with nature

Rituals are a way to bring intention, presence, and mindfulness into your daily life. In nature, rituals help anchor you to the cycles of the Earth, honour the living world, and cultivate a sense of reverence and calm. These practices don't have to be complicated, they can be as simple as pausing to notice a sunrise, honouring a tree, or acknowledging the life around you.

Nature rituals help you:
- Deepen awareness and presence.
- Honor your connection to the natural world.
- Reduce stress and cultivate calm.
- Integrate mindfulness into everyday life.

<u>In-Nature Practice – Morning or Evening Ritual</u>

Begin or end your day with intention and connection.

- Choose a quiet outdoor space, even a small garden, park, or balcony.
- Begin with a few deep breaths, feeling the air on your skin and the ground beneath your feet.
- Observe your surroundings: sounds, scents, colours, and movement.
- Choose a small gesture to honour the moment:
    - Touch a tree or plant gently.
    - Offer a silent word of gratitude.
    - Place a small natural object (stone, leaf, feather) in a personal altar or journal.
- Spend 5–10 minutes in quiet presence, allowing yourself to simply be in nature.
- Journal your experience, noting how it felt and any insights or emotions that arose.

<u>At-Home Practice - Indoor Nature Ritual</u>

Create a mindful connection to nature inside your home.

- Select a natural object or small collection (stones, shells, plants, or water).
- Place them in a dedicated spot or altar.
- Take a few slow breaths, focusing on the textures, colours, and energy of the objects.
- Light a candle, play soft natural sounds, or sit quietly as a daily ritual.
- Reflect and journal about your connection to these objects and the sense of calm or focus they bring.

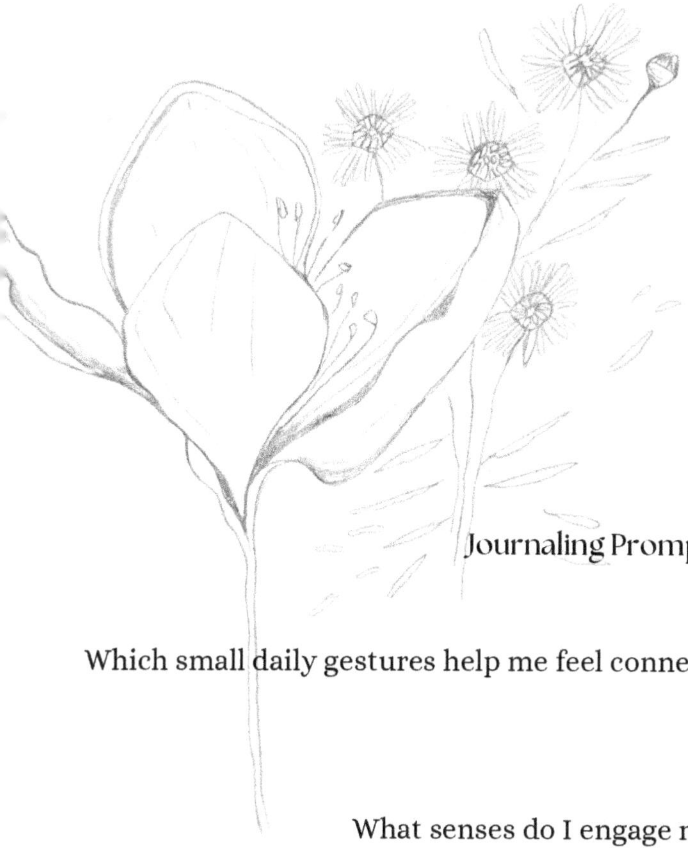

Journaling Prompts - Nature Rituals

Which small daily gestures help me feel connected to the natural world?

What senses do I engage most in my rituals?

How do these rituals affect my mood, focus, or creativity?

Are there seasonal or environmental cues I can incorporate into my rituals?

What natural objects, places, or sounds feel sacred or meaningful to me?

How can I expand these rituals into other areas of my life?

Practice 42 – Connecting to Your Inner Child

Rediscovering playfulness, curiosity, and wonder through nature

Your inner child is the part of you that is curious, playful, and full of wonder. As adults, responsibilities, routines, and stress often push this part of ourselves aside. Nature provides a gentle invitation to reconnect, to explore freely, notice small miracles, and approach life with curiosity and joy.

Connecting with your inner child in nature can:

- Rekindle curiosity and imagination.
- Reduce stress and promote emotional resilience.
- Encourage play and creativity.
- Strengthen a sense of presence and connection to life.

This practice invites you to engage with your inner child through exploration, play, and mindful attention in the natural world. They are still alive inside, you simply just grew around them.

In-Nature Practice – Playful Exploration

Rekindle wonder, curiosity, and joy

- Find a natural space: a park, forest, garden, or even your backyard.

- Approach it as if you were a child seeing it for the first time.

- Engage your senses fully:

  - Touch textures, leaves, and stones.

  - Listen carefully to birds, insects, and rustling leaves.

  - Observe colours, patterns, and movement with curiosity.

- Allow yourself to play, skip stones, collect interesting objects, climb small trees (yep you heard right), or make patterns with natural materials.

- Pause frequently to notice what excites or surprises you.

At-Home Practice - Inner Child Journaling

Reflect on childhood curiosity, imagination, and joy.

- Sit quietly in a safe, comfortable space.

- Close your eyes and recall a childhood memory in nature, real or imagined.

- Write about it in your journal:

  - What did you see, hear, feel, smell, or taste?

  - What made you feel excited or joyful?

  - What did you wonder about?

- Include drawings, doodles, or playful sketches if it helps capture the feeling.

Journaling Prompts - Inner Child Connection

What does my inner child need from me right now?

When was the last time I felt curious, playful, or amazed?

What activities in nature make me feel carefree and joyful?

Which childhood memories in nature still bring me happiness?

How can I invite more play and wonder into my daily life?

Are there natural spaces that feel magical or comforting to me?

Practice 43 – What Do We Want to Remember?

Capturing meaningful moments, lessons, and experiences from nature and life

Life moves quickly, and sometimes the moments that matter most can slip by unnoticed. Taking time to reflect on what we want to remember helps us pause, notice, and honour experiences that shape us. Nature provides a perfect setting to slow down, observe, and connect with memory, meaning, and gratitude.

This practice encourages you to notice what is significant, record it, and allow these memories to become anchors for presence, growth, and joy. Remembering doesn't just preserve the past, it helps us understand ourselves, our choices, and our connection to the world.

By intentionally remembering, you can:
- Recognise meaningful experiences in nature and life.
- Deepen gratitude and appreciation.
- Strengthen personal reflection and mindfulness.
- Create a record of growth, joy, and lessons learned.

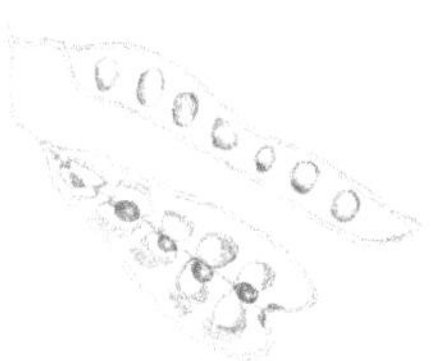

In-Nature Practice – Memory Walk

Notice moments worth remembering during a mindful walk

- Choose a natural setting: forest, beach, park, or garden.
- Walk slowly, paying attention to sights, sounds, and sensations.
- Ask yourself: "What moment here do I want to remember?"
- Pause when something captures your attention: a bird song, sunlight through leaves, the smell of earth after rain, or the texture of bark.
- Journal or take small notes to capture your observations, emotions, or thoughts.

At-Home Practice - Memory Mapping

Reflect on what matters and preserve meaningful experiences

- Find a quiet space indoors.
- Close your eyes and recall a recent outdoor experience, or a moment in daily life, that felt significant.
- Journal about it:
  - What happened?
  - How did it make you feel?
  - Why do you want to remember it?
- Optionally, create a visual map or drawing of the memory, colours, shapes, or symbols that capture the feeling.
- Add these reflections to a "Memory Collection" in your journal.

Journaling Prompts - Remembering Moments

What experiences in nature have made me feel truly alive or present?

Which lessons or insights from the past week do I want to carry forward?

Are there ordinary moments that hold extraordinary meaning?

What sights, sounds, or sensations in nature leave a lasting impression?

How can I honour these memories in my daily life?

Which moments bring me joy or gratitude that I want to remember?

Practice 44 – Where Did I Come From?

Exploring origins, ancestry, and connection to the natural world

Understanding where we come from can deepen our sense of identity, belonging, and purpose. This isn't just about human ancestry, it's also about recognising our connection to the larger web of life, the cycles of nature, and the forces that shape us.

Reflecting on your origins can help you:

- Connect with your personal and family history.
- Recognise the continuity between past and present.
- Appreciate the interconnection of all life.
- Feel grounded and anchored in your place in the world.

This practice encourages you to explore both your human lineage and your connection to nature's ancestry, the generations of life that have led to your existence.

In-Nature Practice – Roots & Lineage Walk

Connect with ancestry and the continuity of life

- Find a natural place with trees, plants, or water.

- Observe roots, branches, or flowing water as symbols of connection and continuity.

- Reflect on questions like:

  - Where do I come from: family, community, nature?

  - Which ancestors or aspects of the past shape who I am today?

  - How does the life around me reflect cycles of growth, decay, and renewal?

- Journal what comes up: thoughts, memories, or insights.

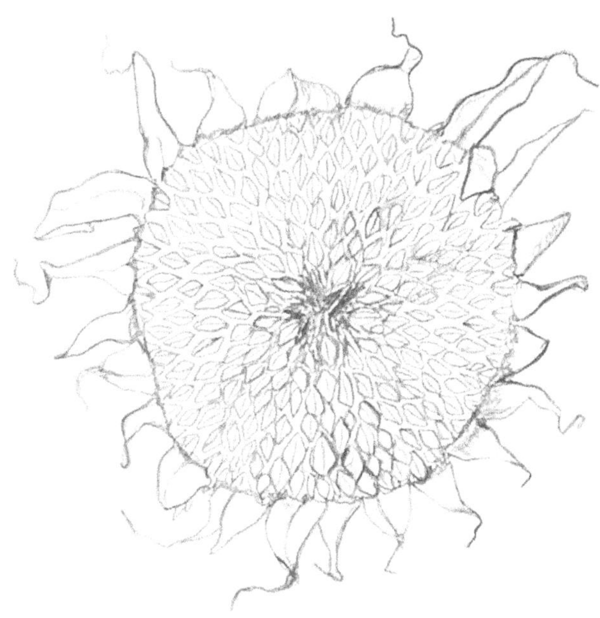

At-Home Practice - Mapping My Origins

Explore personal and ecological ancestry

- Sit quietly with a journal and map out your lineage, memories, or family stories.
- Include:
    - People who influenced you.
    - Places that shaped your upbringing.
    - Traditions or habits passed down.
- Expand the reflection to nature:
    - What natural cycles or environments have shaped your sense of self?
    - Which local species, plants, or landscapes feel like part of your story?
- Draw or create symbols representing your personal and ecological roots.

Journaling Prompts - Exploring Origins

Who or what shaped the person I am today?

Which natural cycles or environments feel like they have influenced me?

What traditions, habits, or values have been passed down to me?

How do I feel connected to the past, present, and future?

Which aspects of my ancestry or origin bring me pride, joy, or curiosity?

How can I honour my roots while growing into my own self?

Practice 45 – Following Your Path

Recognising signs, intuition, and guidance to create your own journey

Life is a journey, and each of us has a path uniquely our own. Following that path requires awareness, courage, and trust: trust in yourself, in the lessons around you, and in the natural guidance life offers.

Nature provides subtle signs and reflections that can help you recognise where to go next. Observing, listening, and reflecting allows you to align with your inner calling and take inspired action.

This chapter helps you notice:
- Inner nudges, curiosity, or excitement.
- Patterns in experiences or relationships.
- Repeated symbols, messages, or opportunities.
- Times of ease versus resistance.

By noticing these signals, you can make decisions that honour your unique purpose and life path.

<u>In-Nature Practice – Pathway Observation</u>

Connect with intuition and natural signs to guide your journey.

- Take a slow walk outdoors, ideally somewhere with natural trails or open spaces.

- Observe your surroundings as if they are speaking to you:
  - Which paths do you feel drawn to?
  - Are there recurring patterns or symbols (leaves, stones, animals) that catch your attention?
  - How does your body feel when you notice these things: relaxed, excited, hesitant?

- Pause and journal about what you notice, both externally in nature and internally in your feelings and thoughts.

At-Home Practice - Signs and Signals Journal

Record guidance from both inner and outer sources

- Reflect on recent experiences that felt meaningful, exciting, or uncomfortable.
- Ask yourself:
    - What repeated patterns or lessons appear in my life?
    - What choices bring me joy and energy versus resistance and tension?
    - Are there symbols, messages, or "coincidences" that feel like guidance?
- Journal your insights, thoughts, and any inspirations for next steps on your path.
- Optionally, create a visual representation, arrows, paths, or symbols that represent your direction.

Journaling Prompts - Recognising Your Path

Which choices or experiences feel aligned with my true self?

What patterns or signs have appeared repeatedly in my life?

When do I feel energised and inspired versus drained and resistant?

Are there symbols or objects in nature that feel like messages for me?

How can I trust my intuition to guide my next steps?

What small actions today can move me along the path I want to create?

Practice 46 – What Do I Need to Let Go Of?

Releasing what no longer serves you to create space for growth

Holding on to old thoughts, habits, or attachments can weigh us down, keeping us from moving forward on our path. Letting go doesn't mean forgetting or denying experiences; it means acknowledging them, learning from them, and choosing not to carry unnecessary burdens into your present or future.

Nature provides a clear model for release: leaves fall in autumn, rivers flow past obstacles, and old growth nourishes new life.

Observing and practicing letting go can help you:

- Release mental or emotional clutter.
- Reduce stress and tension.
- Open space for new experiences and creativity.
- Align more fully with your true path.

<u>In-Nature Practice – Letting Go Walk</u>

Connect with natural cycles of release and renewal

- Take a slow walk in a natural space, ideally where you can observe changing elements (falling leaves, flowing water, wind).
- As you walk, notice anything you feel ready to release:
    - Thoughts, worries, fears, or old beliefs.
    - Habits, relationships, or patterns that no longer serve you.
- Imagine placing these burdens into the natural elements around you:
    - Let leaves or pebbles symbolise what you release.
    - Imagine the wind carrying your worries away.
    - Watch a stream flow past as a metaphor for letting go.
- Journal after, write down what you chose to release and how it feels.

At-Home Practice - Releasing Ritual

Create a personal practice for letting go

- Find a quiet space indoors.
- Write down anything you feel ready to release on small pieces of paper.
- Options for release:
  - Safely burn the papers in a candle flame (symbolising transformation.)
  - Tear them into small pieces and compost them into the Earth.
  - Place them in a bowl of water and watch the paper soften and dissolve.
- Reflect in your journal about what changed emotionally, mentally, or spiritually.

Journaling Prompts - Releasing What No Longer Serves

What thoughts, beliefs, or habits are weighing me down?

Are there relationships or patterns I need to release for my wellbeing?

What does freedom from this feel like?

How can I create space for new experiences by letting go?

Which natural elements or metaphors help me visualise release?

What small daily actions can help me practice letting go?

Practice 47 – Noticing the Signs

Recognising guidance from your environment, intuition, and life to stay aligned with your path

Life often gives us subtle signals when we are moving in alignment or when we are veering off course. These signs can appear in many forms: patterns in nature, repeated experiences, unexpected opportunities, or even quiet nudges from your intuition.

Noticing signs isn't about magic, it's about cultivating awareness. When you pay attention, you begin to see guidance that has always been present. Nature is a perfect teacher, showing us patterns, cycles, and clues about timing and direction.

By learning to notice these signs, you can:
- Make more aligned choices in daily life.
- Trust your intuition and inner wisdom.
- Feel more connected and purposeful.
- Recognise lessons before they become challenges.

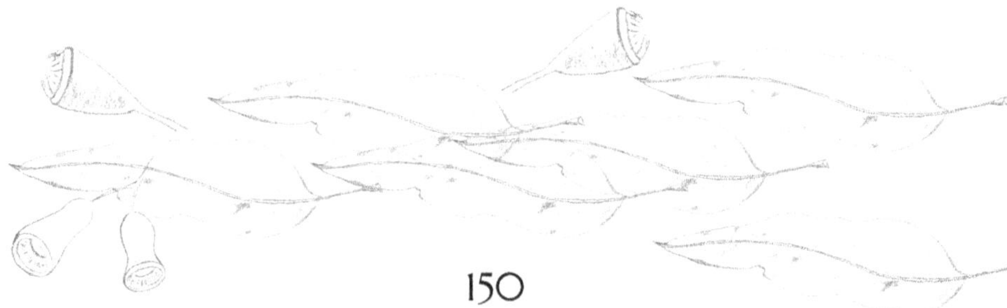

In-Nature Practice – Signs Walk

Observe natural cues as metaphors and guidance for your path

- Take a slow walk outdoors in a natural space.
- As you walk, notice:
  - Animals, plants, or weather patterns that catch your attention.
  - Repeated occurrences or symbols (a bird appearing frequently, patterns in leaves, a stone in a particular shape.)
  - How your body and mind react, curiosity, calm, excitement, hesitation.
- Reflect on whether these signs might mirror experiences, decisions, or emotions in your life.
- Journal your observations: what you noticed, how it made you feel, and any insights about your path.

At-Home Practice - Signs Journal

Capture patterns, nudges, and symbolic guidance from daily life

- Keep a journal specifically for signs and guidance.
- Note:
    - Repeating thoughts or ideas.
    - Patterns in people, events, or nature.
    - Dreams, intuitive feelings, or sudden inspirations.
- Ask: "What could this sign be showing me about my path?"
- Reflect on how these signs might inform your choices or next steps.
- Always thank whoever you believe in for the messages and signs.

Journaling Prompts - Recognising Signs

Which events, symbols, or patterns have appeared repeatedly in my life?

How does my body or intuition respond when I notice these signs?

Are there lessons or messages I've been overlooking?

What opportunities have appeared that I initially ignored?

How can I practice noticing guidance in ordinary moments?

Which signs feel like encouragement, and which feel like caution?

Practice 48 – Symbolic Guidance

Recognising and interpreting personal symbols in nature as guidance

The world around us communicates in subtle ways. Objects, animals, plants, and patterns often appear repeatedly in our lives, acting as symbols that carry meaning or guidance.

Paying attention to these symbols can help us:

- Understand our own thoughts, feelings, and instincts.
- Receive gentle nudges toward growth or action.
- Recognise the lessons life is offering.
- Deepen our connection with the natural world.

Symbolic guidance is not about superstition; it's about noticing patterns, trusting intuition, and exploring meaning in the natural world.

In-Nature Practice – Finding Your Symbols

Observe and record symbols in nature that feel personally significant.

- Take a slow walk or sit quietly in a natural space.
- Open yourself to noticing:
    - Animals that appear repeatedly or catch your attention.
    - Objects like feathers, stones, or flowers.
    - Patterns in leaves, bark, clouds, or water.
- Ask yourself:
    - "Why does this symbol feel meaningful to me?"
    - "What emotions, thoughts, or memories does it evoke?"
    - "Could this symbol be offering guidance about my current situation?"
- Collect these observations in your journal, sketch them, describe them, and write down any insights.

At-Home Practice - Personal Symbol Map

Identify recurring symbols and their meanings in your life.

- Review your past journal entries or reflect on recent experiences.

- Note recurring symbols: animals, objects, natural elements, or even colours shapes and numbers.

- Reflect on their personal meaning:

  - How do they relate to your emotions or experiences?

  - What guidance or reminder might they offer?

- Create a "symbol map":

  - Draw or list each symbol.

  - Write a short reflection about its meaning and guidance.

Journaling Prompts - Interpreting Symbols

Which symbols have appeared repeatedly in my life or surroundings?

What personal meaning or message do these symbols carry?

How do I feel when I encounter these symbols?

Are there lessons or reminders I need to pay attention to?

How can I use these symbols to guide choices or actions?

Can I notice patterns in the timing or location of these symbols?

Practice 49 – Synchronicity & Flow

Recognising meaningful coincidences and moments of effortless alignment

Sometimes life feels as if it "flows" perfectly, and events align in unexpected ways. These moments of synchronicity, when coincidences carry meaning or guidance can be powerful indicators that you are on the right path.

Synchronicity is a gentle reminder that the universe (or life, or nature) responds when you are present, attentive, and aligned with your values.

Noticing these moments helps you:

- Trust your intuition and inner guidance.
- Feel more connected to the world around you.
- Recognise patterns and opportunities you might otherwise overlook.
- Move with life rather than against it.

Flow is the feeling of effortless engagement: when time seems to expand or contract, and you feel fully alive and absorbed in what you are doing. Both flow and synchronicity invite you to pay attention and align with your unique path.

In-Nature Practice – Flow Walk

Experience and notice moments of alignment in nature.

- Take a slow walk in a natural space, ideally somewhere you can observe movement and life (a park, forest, riverbank, or beach).
- Allow your senses to guide you: notice sounds, sights, textures, and scents.
- Pay attention to moments that feel "right" or effortless:
  - Birds appearing exactly when you notice them.
  - Leaves falling in a way that captures your attention.
  - Light or shadows aligning with your path.
- Reflect on how these moments mirror experiences in your life and journal your observations.

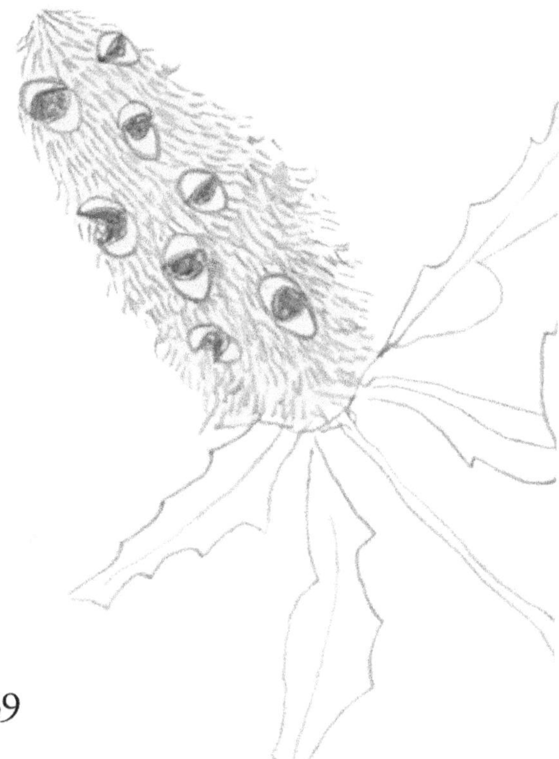

At-Home Practice - Synchronicity Journal

Track meaningful coincidences and flow moments in daily life.

- Keep a small notebook or journal for recording synchronicities and flow experiences.
- Note:
    - Coincidences that feel significant or timely.
    - Moments when you feel completely absorbed or "in the zone."
    - Times when solutions or ideas arise effortlessly.
- Reflect on patterns and possible guidance:
    - What are these moments teaching you about your path?
    - Are there decisions or opportunities you should consider?
- Review weekly and look for repeated themes or lessons.

Journaling Prompts - Recognising Synchronicity & Flow

When have I noticed events aligning in meaningful ways?

How did these moments make me feel, physically and emotionally?

What patterns or lessons appear repeatedly?

Where in my life am I experiencing effortless engagement or flow?

How can I honour these moments to guide my choices?

What small daily practices help me notice synchronicity more often?

Practice 50 – Awakening Your Inner Energy

Becoming aware of energy within the body and its connection to the natural world

Everything in nature moves, water flows, wind travels, trees draw nutrients from the earth, and the sun radiates warmth. This movement is energy in motion.

Within your body, energy is constantly moving, through your breath, your thoughts, your emotions, and your physical sensations. Yet for many of us, this flow becomes restricted or unnoticed as we move through busy, distracted lives. We may feel tension, fatigue, or disconnection without fully understanding why.

When you begin to slow down and listen, you may notice subtle areas of warmth, tightness, lightness, or heaviness. These are gentle signals, your body's way of communicating where energy is flowing freely and where it may need attention.

As you reconnect with nature, you may begin to feel how the energy within you mirrors the world around you, steady like the earth, flowing like water, light like air, warm like the sun.
This practice is about awareness, not perfection. It is about learning to feel again.

<u>In-Nature Practice – Feeling the Flow</u>

Notice how energy moves within your body while connected to nature.

- Find a quiet place outdoors, somewhere you feel comfortable and safe.
- Sit or stand still and take a few slow, gentle breaths.
- Bring your attention into your body. Notice where you feel:
  - Warmth or coolness.
  - Tension or softness.
  - Heaviness or lightness.
- Slowly scan your body from your feet to the top of your head.
- As you do this, imagine your breath moving through you, like water flowing through a river.
- If you notice an area that feels tight or blocked, simply breathe into that space. No need to change it, just bring awareness.
- Now widen your awareness to your surroundings:
  - Feel the ground beneath you.
  - Notice the air on your skin.
  - Listen to the sounds around you.
- Allow yourself to sense how your inner energy and the natural environment feel connected.

<u>At-Home Practice - Gentle Energy Awareness</u>

Build awareness of your body's energy in a simple, accessible way.

- Sit or lie down in a comfortable position.

- Close your eyes and take slow, steady breaths.

- Place one hand on your chest and one on your lower belly.

- Notice the rise and fall of your breath.

- Gently move your awareness through your body:

  - Moving down from the head and over the face.

  - Moving down to the throat and over the neck.

  - Moving into the chest and down your arms.

  - Moving back to the chest, flowing down to the belly.

  - Moving from the belly down into the hips.

  - Letting the energy flow into the legs.

  - Flowing out through the base of your feet.

- At each point, pause and simply notice what you feel.

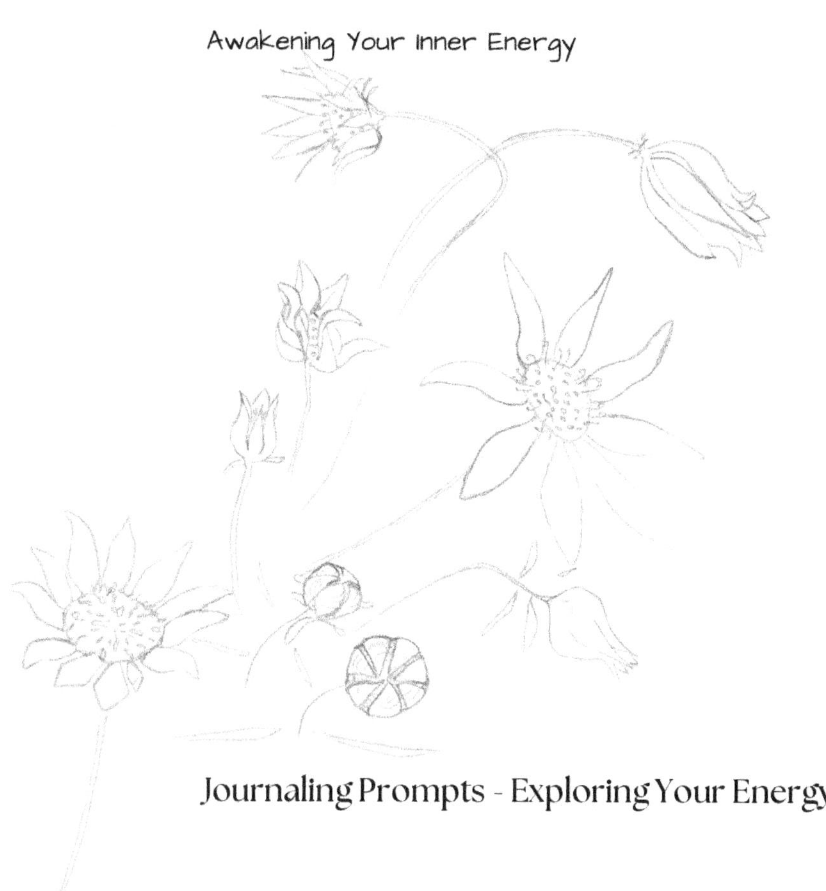

Journaling Prompts - Exploring Your Energy

Where in my body do I feel the most ease right now?

Where do I notice tension or heaviness?

How does my body feel after my energy flowing through me?

What helps me feel more open, calm, or grounded?

What might my body be trying to communicate to me?